Sunset
Microwave Cook Book

By the Editors of Sunset Books and Sunset Magazine

Lane Publishing Co. • Menlo Park, California

How We Tested Our Recipes

The recipes for this new *Sunset Microwave Cook Book* were tested by staff home economists using microwave ovens with full cooking power of 650 watts. Though this is typical of the microwave ovens on the market today, we give a range of time in most recipes to accommodate those ovens with full power that's at a higher or lower wattage. Always check the food for doneness after the minimum amount of time given; then add time, if necessary, to complete cooking.

For most of our testing, we used clear ovenproof glass containers in the appropriate sizes. For coverings we used heavyweight clear plastic wrap, standard wax paper, and white all-paper towels. Our plastic bags were purchased as "cooking bags" and tied with string or a piece of plastic. Shields for food were made of standard-weight aluminum foil.

And the result of all this testing? It's a cook book that we believe will enable you to enjoy microwave cooking as much as we do.

Acknowledgments

We wish to extend a special thank-you to McNett's Microwave for sharing their expertise in microwave cooking. And for their cooperation in providing the kitchenware and decorative accessories that grace our photographs, we thank Agapanthus, House of Today, Taylor & Ng, and Williams-Sonoma Kitchenware.

Edited by Elaine R. Woodard

Special Consultants: **Joan Griffiths**
Ruby Beilby

Design: **Joe di Chiarro**
Photography: **Nikolay Zurek**
Photo Editor: **Lynne B. Morrall**
Illustrations: **Dick Cole**

Front cover: Microwave magic turns out a full, exciting meal in a fraction of the time conventional cooking would take: Game Hens with Apricots (page 38), steamed broccoli spears (page 50), Stuffed Potatoes (page 56), and Spicy Steamed Pudding (page 80). Photographed by Tom Wyatt.

Sunset Books
   Editor, David E. Clark
   Managing Editor, Elizabeth L. Hogan

Seventh printing July 1987

CONTENTS

4   Microwave Magic

12 Hors d'oeuvres & Beverages

20 Meat, Poultry & Fish

48 Vegetables

64 Eggs & Cheese

72 Sweets & Breakfast Treats

90 Sauces—Savory or Sweet

94 Index

Special Features

10 A Miscellany of Microwave Tips
15 Roasted Nuts & Seeds
22 Meat Cooking Chart
24 Fish Cooking Chart
25 Poultry Cooking Chart
33 Hearty Hot Sandwiches
40 Dressing Up the Bird
44 Kids' Korner
49 Fresh Vegetable Cooking Chart
53 Dress Up Your Vegetables
57 Baked Potato Entrées
60 The Soup Tureen
69 Microwave Egg Basics
76 Fresh Fruit Jams
84 The Candy Box
96 Metric Conversion Table

Microwave Magic

Today's microwave cooking — speedy, cool, clean, and energy efficient — opens up a new world of excitement and challenge. That's not to say short cooking times inhibit a relaxed, creative approach to cooking; and don't think you have to forget what you already know about cooking. You're simply adding another dimension.

WHY COOK WITH MICROWAVES?

Microwave cooking saves time — when you're cooking from scratch, when you're thawing frozen foods, and when you're reheating previously cooked foods. Many foods cook by microwaves in about a quarter of the time it would take conventionally. But not all foods cook well in the microwave. Very large quantities, foods that need time to absorb water (like rice and pasta), and foods that need to simmer a long time to become tender are best left to conventional methods.

Not only do many foods cook faster in the microwave, but they also retain more color, flavor, and texture. You'll especially appreciate the way the microwave cooks vegetables — they emerge bright, flavorful, and tender-crisp. Moreover, there's a greater retention of nutrients, especially water soluble vitamins, in microwave cooking.

Since the oven cavity doesn't heat up (except minimally from the food), cooking is cool — no blast of hot air hits you when you open the door to check or remove food. Of course, now you won't have an excuse not to cook on a hot summer day.

Cool cooking also means less clean-up; foods don't burn onto their containers, and spatter (if any) doesn't burn onto the oven surface. Because most foods are cooked in serving containers, there are rarely any pots and pans to wash. And as an added bonus, the microwave can also save energy because it cooks so quickly.

HOW DOES THE MICROWAVE COOK FOOD?

To understand what the oven can do, you need to know how it works. The heart of the microwave oven is the magnetron tube, which converts ordinary household electricity into high frequency microwaves. The frequency designated by the Federal Communications Commission for use in microwave ovens is 2450 megahertz. This means the waves vibrate about 2½ billion times per second.

When the microwaves reach the oven cavity, they're distributed by a metal-blade stirrer fan. These waves are either reflected, passed through, or absorbed by different materials. Metal reflects microwaves, so the basic wall material and stirrer fan are made of metal. Glass, pottery, paper, plastic, and wax allow the microwaves to pass through — that's why these materials are used for cooking containers and coverings. Cooking containers can pick up heat from the food itself, though, so you'll need pot holders when cooking for long periods.

It's primarily the water in food that absorbs microwaves, but fat and sugar also react to microwave energy. The absorbed microwave energy causes these molecules to vibrate rapidly; the resulting friction causes heat, and that's what cooks the food.

Because the microwaves generally penetrate only ¾ to 1½ inches into the food, the center of a large mass of food — a roast, for example— will be cooked not by microwave energy but by the surrounding heat as it's conducted inward. The depth of microwave penetration depends on the density of the food. Microwaves penetrate deeper into bread than meat, for example, because bread is less dense.

Because the air in the oven is not affected by microwaves, it stays cool, unless laden with steam from the cooking food. A lot of steam can be trapped under tight covers of cooking containers, so be very careful when removing them, and always remove them so the steam will escape away from you.

HOW SAFE ARE MICROWAVE OVENS?

Microwave oven manufacturers must adhere to stringent safety standards set up by the United States Government under the Federal Safety Performance Standards for Microwave Ovens by the Department of Health and Human Services.

Microwaves are nonionizing radiant energy, like radio waves. Unlike ionizing X-rays, microwaves don't cause chemical change, except as heat is created. No ionizing radiation is produced with microwaves; if you were exposed to microwaves, you would feel heat just as the food does.

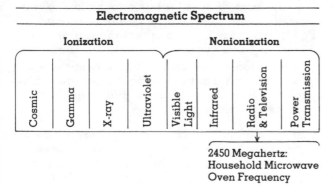

Electromagnetic Spectrum

Ionization: Cosmic, Gamma, X-ray, Ultraviolet

Nonionization: Visible Light, Infrared, Radio & Television, Power Transmission

2450 Megahertz: Household Microwave Oven Frequency

Though pacemakers used to be affected by microwaves as well as by other radio waves, pacemakers now are shielded and aren't bothered by these interferences.

Ovens are carefully designed to contain the microwaves inside the oven cavity. Door seals prevent leakage, and automatic shut-off switches with double or triple interlock systems ensure that no microwave energy is generated when the door is open. Microwaves obey the inverse square law — their intensity drops dramatically as the distance from the source of energy increases. The possibility of your being exposed to an excessive amount of radiant energy is very remote.

Do be sure, though, to follow the manufacturer's instructions for the use and maintenance of your oven, and observe the following precautions:

○ Keep the oven clean, especially around the door seal.

○ Never tamper with the oven in any way.

○ Be sure nothing is ever caught in the door.

If you suspect damage of any kind, do not use the oven until it's been checked by a service representative.

HOW DO MICROWAVE OVENS DIFFER?

As with other major appliances, there's a staggering array of microwave oven models available on the market. But regardless of the design, switches, and special features that distinguish one from the other, every oven is basically a metal box with a magnetron tube, transformer, cooling fan, and controls. A wave guide directs the microwaves into the cavity, where they are distributed by a stirrer fan or a rotating antenna. A metal screen on the door has holes large enough for viewing but small enough to keep the microwaves inside. Vents release steam and moisture.

Still the most popular model, the portable countertop oven can be either on a counter or on a cart. You can also purchase built-in models: a microwave oven can be part of a free-standing double oven where the microwave is at eye level and the conventional oven is below, or it can be installed over a range, incorporating both a light and a vent.

Ovens that combine two completely different cooking methods — microwave and conventional or microwave and convection — allow you to cook in the same oven using the two methods simultaneously or independently.

Cooking power, expressed in wattage, differs from oven to oven, as do the terms used by the manufacturers to express it. Full power varies from 600 to 700 watts. Some less expensive models may have full power of only 450 or 500 watts. The higher the wattage, the faster the food will cook. As this book goes to press, the average full power is 650 watts; this is the wattage we used for full power — or what we call **HIGH (100%)** — when we tested the recipes in this book.

If you don't know the wattage of your oven, place a cup of room-temperature water (72°F/22°C) in a 1-cup glass measure. Place cup on microwave floor. Microwave, uncovered, on **HIGH (100%)** and note the time required to bring the water to a boil (bubbles will break the surface). If the oven is in the 600 to 700-watt range, the water will boil in 2½ to 3 minutes.

Some ovens have a limited number of power choices; others offer a complete range of variable power settings from full power to 10 or 20 percent. Following the standards adopted by the International Microwave Power Institute, we have developed our recipes according to five power designations:

HIGH (100%):	600 to 700 watts
MEDIUM-HIGH (70%):	450 to 490 watts
MEDIUM (50%):	300 to 350 watts
LOW (30%):	180 to 210 watts
WARM (10%):	65 to 130 watts

To prevent any variables from interfering with your microwave oven's cooking performance, put your microwave on its own grounded circuit. If the oven is plugged into a circuit with another large appliance, such as a refrigerator, the electrical voltage coming into the microwave will be low at certain times; you may then have to increase the cooking time beyond that stated in the recipe (bakery products are most affected). When two appliances are on the same circuit and in use simultaneously, it's possible to blow a fuse or trip a circuit breaker.

If you've ever shopped for a microwave, you know that a number of special features are available on the various models. Some have a browning element, an electric unit in the top of the oven cavity designed to brown foods conventionally. In the portable countertop ovens, which run on 115 to 120 volts, the browning element must be used separately from the microwave, either before or after the food is cooked. If you don't have a browning element in your microwave, you can achieve the same effect using your conventional broiler.

Some microwave ovens come with a built-in turntable or carousel, a round tray in the bottom of the oven that rotates the food. Separate battery-operated turntables are now available as an accessory for any oven.

Electronic controls, a feature on some models, allow the cook to program changes in power level. For instance, you may want to defrost meat on low power and then cook on medium-high. With these special controls, you can enter both processes at the same time.

You'll even find ovens equipped with automatic sensing devices that eliminate any uncertainties. A temperature probe inserted into the food signals when the programmed internal temperature has been reached. Some ovens feature auto-sensor programs to detect the humidity level; they automatically determine how long the food should cook, and they signal when the food is done.

The ultimate in automatic programmed devices is the computer card control. The cook places a card with a programmed recipe on it into a slot in the oven, and the oven selects the power level and timing.

MICROWAVE-SAFE UTENSILS & MATERIALS

Always choose a container or material that allows microwave energy to pass through it to reach the food. Glass, pottery, china, paper, and thermoplastic are the most common materials used in the microwave.

Caution. Avoid metal containers or containers with any metallic trims, especially gold and silver, as they reflect the microwaves and can cause arcing in the oven, which would eventually damage the magnetron tube.

Caution. Always choose containers that are colorless and plain; color and decoration can interfere with the transmission of microwaves.

Caution. Never operate your microwave oven unless you have food or liquid in it.

Heatproof glassware, glass-ceramics, and heatproof plastics designed for microwave cooking are your best choices for basic cookware. Whenever possible, use containers that are round. Foods cooked in square or rectangular dishes are likely to be overcooked on the corners.

In addition to casseroles and baking dishes, glass measuring cups of various sizes are indispensable for cooking sauces, puddings, jams, candies, and even artichokes.

Pottery, plastic, and china may or may not be all right to use in the microwave. Some of these may contain materials that interfere with the transmission of microwaves; check with the manufacturer to be certain your dishes are microwave safe.

If you're not certain whether your cookware is safe to use, perform a simple dish test to find out. Fill a glass measure with 1 cup of water and place it in the microwave, alongside the dish in question. Microwave on **HIGH (100%)** for 1 minute. Only the water should get hot. If the dish heats up too, it should not be used in the microwave oven.

Plastic foam plates and cups can be used in your microwave for heating food at low temperatures, but do not use them for actual cooking.

Plastic bags can be used in the microwave, but be sure they are designated as cooking bags—do *not* use plastic bags from the produce department of the grocery store. Also, do *not* use the twist ties accompanying some plastic bags; if you need to tie the bag closed, use a string, a strip of plastic, or a rubber band.

Paper plates, cups, bags, napkins, and towels can be used in the microwave. Plastic-coated paper plates are good for moist foods. Use wax-coated plates at low temperatures, if at all—high temperatures may melt the wax, and colors may bleed or have interfering substances. Newspaper may contain metallic ink and should not be used. Check that your paper towels are all paper; if they're blended with other substances, such as synthetics, they can decompose.

Plastic wrap or glass or ceramic lids are good container covers. For maximum retention of moisture, tightly seal dishes with *heavy-duty plastic wrap* or *glass or ceramic lids*. When you need to allow for expansion, cover with heavy-duty *pleated plastic wrap*, following the folding method illustrated below. When you need only minumum moisture retention, *wax paper* is ideal; the wax also helps to diffuse the microwaves. If moisture needs to be absorbed to prevent food from getting soggy, use *paper towels* as covers.

Note. Whenever we call for plastic wrap, we recommend using the kinds that are specifically

described on the package as being for use in the microwave. Lightweight plastic wraps may split during cooking and melt into the food.

Straw and wood should be given only limited use, such as a basket (without staples) for warming rolls or a wooden spoon left in a sauce for stirring.

Aluminum foil's use in the microwave is controversial. Most oven manufacturers state that a limited amount may be used, like a TV dinner tray (not more than ¾ inch deep) or small pieces to shield parts of food likely to cook too fast. But since there are oven manufacturers who oppose its use, check your owner's manual before you use aluminum foil. If aluminum foil is approved for your oven, don't let it touch the oven walls.

Microwave specialty items. The browning dish or skillet must be preheated, and it heats up at the rate of about 100° per minute. But it loses heat very quickly and usually will not brown both sides of the food equally. Other specialty items include meat racks, trivets, cupcakers, bacon trees, ring molds, thermometers, and a plastic shelf that allows you to put more food in the oven at one time.

SPECIAL TECHNIQUES FOR MICROWAVE COOKING

As in conventional cooking, the starting temperature of the food affects the total cooking time; frozen or refrigerated food will take longer to cook than food at room temperature. But unlike conventional cooking, microwave cooking has a number of additional variables that influence time and results. If you understand these variables, you'll understand the need for the special techniques used in microwave cooking.

Quantity of food. More food means more time. If you double the quantity of food, you'll need to increase the cooking time by about 60 percent. Whenever you vary the quantity in a given recipe, be sure to alter the time accordingly. Unfortunately, though, there's no exact formula.

Uniformity of size and shape. Microwaves penetrate small pieces much faster than larger ones. For even cooking, cut fruit, vegetables, and meat into pieces of uniform size and shape. Individual food items, such as potatoes and apples, should be as nearly alike in size and shape as possible.

Food that is unevenly shaped — chicken pieces, chops, or potatoes tapered at one end —

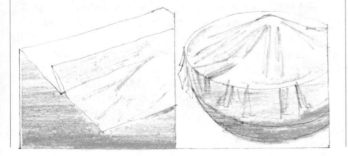

should be placed in a baking dish or on a rack with the thickest portions to the outside of the dish. Vegetables with thick, tough stalks should be arranged with the buds or tips meeting in the center and the tough stem ends to the outside of the dish.

Composition of the food.   Denser food, such as meat, will take longer to cook than less-dense food of equal size. The amount of liquid in the food is also a factor in the cooking time. Moist parts will get hotter than drier parts. For example, a sandwich filling will get hotter than the bread, because moisture absorbs microwaves so readily; remember to test the filling for temperature, and not just the bread.

Whenever excess liquid accumulates in the bottom of a roasting container, use a bulb baster to remove the drippings. Otherwise, the liquid will absorb microwaves and reduce cooking efficiency. Foods high in fat and sugar get very hot in the microwave oven, so watch them carefully and use pot holders when removing them from the oven.

Arrangement of food.   When cooking a number of items (up to eight) like potatoes, individual eggs, or muffins, place them in a circle for more even cooking. The diagram below shows the ideal placement of one to eight items; never put anything in the center of a circle. Leave about an inch of space between items for efficient microwave penetration, and always arrange them in a single layer rather than on top of each other.

Stirring, rotating, and rearranging.   Since microwaves penetrate a limited distance and most ovens cook somewhat unevenly, you'll get better results with some foods — especially large sizes and quantities — if you stir, rotate, or rearrange them. (To check the evenness of the heating pattern in your oven, place a wet piece of smooth brown paper, the size of your oven floor, in the oven and microwave it on **HIGH (100%)** for 1 minute. Notice where the paper is still damp. In those areas, the food will take longer to cook.)

Directions for stirring, rotating, or rearranging

food are given in each recipe when necessary. Stirring is extremely important for making sauces. Rotating a baking dish may sometimes be avoided if you cover the container and/or use lower power settings. Occasionally, shifting the position of the food in the oven — such as raising the container off the oven floor by placing it on an inverted saucer — evens out the cooking. We found this technique worked well in some ovens for cakes and bar cookies.

Standing time.   This is extremely important in microwave cooking. Since the microwaves are vibrating at about 2½ billion times per second, the molecules in the food do not stop immediately when the microwave oven is turned off. It takes time for them to slow down, so cooking continues even after the food is no longer being exposed to the microwaves. Many foods will continue to cook for 5 to 20 more minutes. Standing time is particularly important for large, dense food items like roasts.

Standing times and doneness tests appear in all the recipes in this book. Remember — it's better to undercook food and add more cooking time later than to have the food overcook.

Added seasonings and color.   Because salt draws liquid out of food and interferes with the microwave cooking pattern, never sprinkle meat or vegetables with salt until after they're microwaved. Other seasonings can be used when desired. Since microwaved foods do not brown (except when fats become very hot, as with some meats), you may want to use a sauce, baste, or topping to color your food and enhance its appearance. Dark brown sugar, Cheddar cheese, and bottled brown gravy sauce will become staples in your kitchen. You'll use all of these in our recipes, which have been developed for their eye appeal as well as their taste appeal.

DEFROSTING FOOD IN THE MICROWAVE

Who hasn't at one time or another wished for a magic spell that, recited over a solidly frozen chunk of food, would thaw it in the wink of an eye? Well, we can't give you any magic incantations, but we can tell you that the microwave works almost as well.

Though you can defrost at any power level, a low power is recommended so the food won't begin to cook on the outside before it has thawed on the inside. Many ovens have a setting labeled "defrost," usually designated about half or one-third power; typically, the power cycles on and off. You'll need to remove the frozen item and let it stand the same amount of time it was microwaved. For example, to thaw a roast, microwave it for 5 minutes, then allow it 5 minutes of standing time. This allows the heat to penetrate without cooking the outside.

Distributing the heating effect of the microwaves evenly is the key to defrosting. Use the following techniques to help achieve even heating.

○ If it's wrapped in paper or plastic, leave the food in the package to begin defrosting. If it's foil-wrapped, remove the wrapping and place the food in a glass container.

○ Cover the dish with wax paper — this helps to diffuse the microwaves.

○ Separate the pieces as soon as possible so all the edges can be exposed. Leave plenty of space between pieces, and place the thicker portions to the outside.

○ Stir, break up with a fork, rotate, and rearrange the food, if possible.

○ Remove portions as they thaw so all the energy will be directed to the still-frozen parts.

Though published guides may tell you how long to defrost a given item, you still need to check fairly frequently and follow the techniques above for best results. For example, a pound of ground beef left in its wrappings will defrost in about 5 minutes at **MEDIUM (50%),** but you'll need to stop after about 3 minutes, unwrap the package, break up the meat with a fork as much as possible, and remove already thawed meat. If you start by unwrapping the frozen meat, placing it in a glass dish, and covering it with wax paper, it will be easier to break up. Let it stand, covered, for 5 minutes. The meat should still be slightly icy.

TECHNIQUES FOR REHEATING FOOD

With a microwave, your family need never know that the meal they're consuming with such relish is actually another day's leftovers. That's how well the microwave preserves the food's original taste and appearance. And if you use glass, plastic, or paper, you can store, reheat, and even serve out of the same container.

Leftovers from the refrigerator will generally take about 2 minutes on **HIGH (100%)** for each cup of food to reach serving temperature. Stir the food halfway through the cooking time if you have more than 2 cups. Always cover leftovers during reheating — wax paper is ideal.

When arranging a plate for a meal of leftovers, put the thicker portions to the outside of the plate. Don't reheat a leftover roll or slice of bread with the other foods on the plate. Breads, very light in density, heat very fast and easily become dry and tough. Add the roll during the last 15 seconds of heating.

If, after you've cooked a meal, you need to refrigerate a plate for someone who's arriving late, cover the plate with plastic wrap. When you're ready to serve it, simply pop the dish, cover and all, into the microwave for 1 or 2 minutes.

A little microwaving does wonders to refresh purchased sweet rolls, doughnuts, and other bakery products. Single items will get hot in about 15 seconds on **HIGH (100%)**. A plate of 6 to 8 sweet rolls takes about 1½ minutes. Wrap bread and dinner rolls loosely in a paper towel or napkin or heat them in a basket (be sure there are no staples) with a cloth napkin.

Treat canned foods like reheated food; food in cans has already been cooked and needs only to be heated to serving temperature. Place the canned food in a microwave-safe dish, cover it, and follow the guideline of 2 minutes for each cup, stirring if necessary.

FOODS THAT MICROWAVE WELL — AND THOSE THAT DON'T

Though a microwave oven may not be the answer to all your cooking needs, once you've tried some of our recipes and techniques, you'll wonder how you ever got along without one. You'll especially appreciate the exceptional results you'll get when you microwave vegetables, fruits, casseroles, jams, bacon, fish, chicken, and many appetizers. Heating sandwiches and beverages is a snap. Soup, in small quantities, cooks easily, and candy-making is temptingly quick.

Meat, eggs, cheese, and other foods high in protein need to be microwaved carefully, usually at lower power, to prevent the protein from becoming tough. Bread, cakes, and some other bakery products are generally less satisfactory baked in a microwave than in a conventional oven, though the number of successful microwave recipes is steadily increasing.

The microwave is not designed for large items and large quantities of food. These are better cooked conventionally. Also unsuccessful in the microwave are foods that depend heavily on air beaten into eggs for leavening, like angel food cakes and popovers; these require dry heat to cook. The microwave cannot fry foods, with the exception of limited items in the browning dish, nor does it toast or crust food.

If you're not already convinced of the versatility of your microwave oven, just glance at the quick tips presented below. Then enjoy the convenient and carefree cooking your oven provides. The times are approximate.

○ **Softening hardened brown sugar.** Put a few drops of water (or a wedge of apple) into the box of hardened sugar. Close the box and microwave on **HIGH (100%)** for 15 to 20 seconds per cup of sugar or until lumps soften. Let stand for 5 minutes. (If the sugar is packaged in a foil-lined container, place the sugar in a glass dish, cover it with wax paper, and microwave it as above.)

○ **Melting a cube of butter or margarine.** Place 1 cube (½ cup) butter, unwrapped, in a 10-ounce custard cup or dish. Microwave, uncovered, on **HIGH (100%)** for 1 minute.

○ **Softening a cube of butter or margarine.** Place 1 cube (½ cup) butter, unwrapped, on a saucer. Microwave, uncovered, on **MEDIUM (50%)** for 10 to 15 seconds. Let stand 5 minutes to complete softening.

○ **Softening cream cheese.** Unwrap 1 small package (3 oz.) cream cheese and place it in a 10-ounce custard cup or dish. Cover it with wax paper. Microwave on **MEDIUM (50%)** for ½ to 1 minute. For a large package (8 oz.), microwave, covered, on **MEDIUM (50%)** for 1½ to 2 minutes.

○ **Melting a 1-ounce square of chocolate.** Place 1 square (1 oz.) chocolate, unwrapped, in a small dish. Cover it with wax paper. Microwave on **MEDIUM (50%)** for 2 to 2½ minutes or until softened. Stir until thoroughly melted. Do not overheat or the chocolate will scorch around the edges and won't blend smoothly.

○ **Heating instant cocoa.** For each serving of cocoa, combine in a mug or cup sweetened cocoa mix and milk in the proportions suggested on the package. Microwave, uncovered, on **HIGH (100%)** for 1½ to 2 minutes or until heated through. Add a marshmallow, if desired, the last 20 seconds of heating.

○ **Uncrystallizing honey or jam.** Remove the metal lid from the glass jar. Place the container on the oven floor. Microwave, uncovered, on **HIGH (100%)** for 1 to 1½ minutes per cup of honey or jam or until the sugar crystals have melted.

○ **Warming tortillas and crêpes.** To soften an unopened package of tortillas, make a slit in the package and place it on the oven floor. Microwave on **HIGH (100%)** for 1 minute. Or wrap the number of tortillas or crêpes you need in paper towels. Microwave on **HIGH (100%)** for 6 to 7 seconds per piece.

○ **Reaming more juice from citrus fruits.** Place a lemon, orange, or grapefruit on the oven floor. Microwave on **HIGH (100%)** for about 15 seconds. Roll the fruit between your palms a few times; then cut the fruit and squeeze out the juices.

○ **Softening ice cream for easier serving.** Place unopened ½ gallon hard ice cream on the oven floor. Microwave on **MEDIUM (50%)** for 45 seconds to 1 minute. Let it stand for a few minutes before serving.

○ **Cutting winter squash.** The tough outer skins of acorn, butternut, and spaghetti squash are often hard to cut. For easier cutting, place the squash on the oven floor. Microwave, uncovered, on **HIGH (100%)** for 1 to 2 minutes. Let it stand for 1 to 2 minutes before cutting.

○ **Boiling water.** For 1 cup, place water in a bowl or glass measure. Microwave, uncovered, on **HIGH (100%)** for 2½ to 3 minutes or until tiny bubbles break the surface. If you need more than a cup of boiling water, you'll save time by heating it on the range.

○ **Heating prepared soups.** From packet or can to steaming mug or bowl, it's a snap.

For an individual-serving-size package of dry soup mix, pour ¾ cup hot tap water (or the amount specified on the package) into a cup or mug. Microwave, uncovered, on **HIGH (100%)** for 2 to 3 minutes or until the water boils. Slowly stir in 1 package (about 1½ oz.) dry soup mix. Stir until the mixture has dissolved.

For dry soup mix, stir together 1 package or envelope of instant soup mix (amount for 3 or 4 servings) and 4 cups hot tap water (or the amount specified on the package) in a 2-quart soup tureen or casserole. Cover with a lid or wax paper. Microwave on **HIGH (100%)** for about 10 minutes (stirring every 3 minutes) or until the soup is hot and bubbly. Let it stand, covered, for 2 to 3 minutes; stir well before serving. Makes 3 or 4 servings.

For a single serving of condensed soup, fill a mug or bowl a little less than half full with the soup; gradually stir in an equal amount of hot tap water. Microwave, uncovered, on **HIGH (100%)** for 2 to 3 minutes or until the soup is hot and bubbly.

For an entire can of condensed soup, spoon the can of soup into a deep 1-quart casserole; gradually stir in an equal amount of hot tap water. Cover with a lid or wax paper. Microwave on **HIGH (100%)** for 6 to 8 minutes (stirring every 3 minutes) or until hot and bubbly.

○ **Heating a jar of baby food.** Remove the metal lid from 1 jar (4½ oz.) baby food (at room temperature). Place the jar on the oven floor. Microwave, uncovered, on **HIGH (100%)** for 15 to 20 seconds or until warm. Stir and test for warmth

before serving. If the jar has been refrigerated, microwave, uncovered, on **HIGH (100%)** for about 15 seconds per ounce of food.

○ **Heating a baby bottle.** Fill a bottle with 4 ounces of milk or formula. Place the bottle with the nipple attached on the oven floor. Microwave on **HIGH (100%)** for 15 to 20 seconds. Shake the bottle and test the milk's temperature on your wrist. If the bottle has been refrigerated, microwave on **HIGH (100%)** for 40 to 50 seconds. Shake the bottle and test the milk.

○ **Reheating refrigerated casserole-type leftovers.** Store your leftover food in a microwave-safe container. To reheat the food, cover the container with a lid or wax paper. Microwave on **HIGH (100%)** for 2 minutes (stirring, if possible, after 1 minute) per cup of refrigerated food.

○ **Reheating a plate of room-temperature food.** Place dense or thick portions to the outside edge of the plate. Arrange light, delicate foods like mashed potatoes or vegetables in the center of the plate. Cover it with wax paper. Microwave on **HIGH (100%)** for 1 to 1½ minutes or until heated through.

○ **Heating finger towels.** For a quick clean-up after eating messy food, wet small finger towels and wring out the excess moisture. Sprinkle them lightly with lemon juice, roll them up individually, and microwave on **HIGH (100%)** for about 30 seconds per towel.

○ **Heating coffee, tea, and cider.** To reheat a cup of room-temperature coffee, microwave on **HIGH (100%)** for 1 to 1½ minutes or until it's heated through. Or stir about 1 teaspoon instant coffee into a cup or mug, fill it with water, and microwave as above. For tea, simply place water in a cup or mug. Microwave on **HIGH (100%)** for 1 to 1½ minutes; then drop in a tea bag or a ball of spiced tea and let the tea steep until it's at the desired strength. To heat cider, place 1 cup cold cider and 1 whole cinnamon stick in a cup or mug. Microwave on **HIGH (100%)** for 1½ to 2 minutes or until heated through.

○ **Making croutons.** Place 4 tablespoons butter or margarine in a 7 by 11-inch baking dish. Microwave, uncovered, on **HIGH (100%)** for 1 minute. Stir in about 4 cups fresh bread cubes and dried herbs, if desired. Microwave, uncovered, on **HIGH (100%)** for 4 to 6 minutes, stirring every minute. Let the croutons stand for 5 minutes to harden completely.

Hors d'oeuvres & Beverages

Here we offer nourishing snacks, tantalizing hors d'oeuvres, and instantly heated beverages — once you've prepared some of these, you'll wonder if the microwave oven was invented expressly for them. Whether you're appeasing sudden hunger pangs or serving unexpected company, our recipes allow hassle-free spontaneity.

TIPS & TECHNIQUES

○ **Melting cheese.** Jack, fontina, teleme, Swiss, Longhorn Cheddar, and all process cheese spread on crackers or stirred into dips and fondue melt quickly in the microwave. Even after the cheese has cooled it can be reheated on **MEDIUM (50%)** to a smooth and creamy consistency.

○ **Softening refrigerated cheese.** For easier slicing of refrigerated cheese, cover the cheese with plastic wrap and place it directly on the floor of the microwave. Microwave on **MEDIUM (50%)** for 30 seconds to 1 minute (depending on size) or until cheese is slightly soft to the touch.

○ **Canapés.** Though you can prepare the toppings for canapés in advance, don't spread the toppings on their crisp bases until just before you're ready to heat them or they'll become soggy. Be sure to serve the canapés immediately after they're microwaved to prevent the base from softening (see Pepperoni Pizza Rounds, page 16). For canapé bases, use Melba toast rounds or shredded wheat crackers, thin wheat crackers, or crisp rye crackers.

○ **Crisping stale snacks.** Don't throw out those stale chips!

Line a plate or wicker basket (without metal staples) with paper towels. Add 2 to 3 cups stale potato chips, corn chips, pretzels, crackers, or popcorn. Microwave, uncovered, on **HIGH (100%)** for 30 seconds to 1 minute. Let them stand for 3 to 4 minutes until crisp.

○ **Microwaving appetizers for a crowd.** Microwaving a large batch of appetizers will take more time than cooking the appetizers conventionally. If you need appetizers for a crowd, bake them all at once in your conventional oven. Then simply reheat small batches in the microwave so you can offer them piping hot.

○ **Hot bouillon.** Drop a bouillon cube or a teaspoon of stock base in a 6-ounce cup or mug filled with tap water. Microwave, uncovered, on **HIGH (100%)** for 1½ minutes (stirring after 1 minute) or until bouillon has dissolved and mixture is steaming hot. Add a thin slice of lemon to each cup for zest.

○ **Hot coffee or tea.** Why leave your coffeepot plugged in all day? Just brew a pot of coffee early in the day and then, when you want a cup later on, reheat it in the microwave on **HIGH (100%)** for 1 to 1½ minutes. Or add about 1 teaspoon instant coffee to a 6-ounce cup or mug filled with tap water and microwave on **HIGH (100%)** for 1 to 1½ minutes or until steaming hot. For tea, simply place water in a 6-ounce cup or mug and microwave on **HIGH (100%)** for 1 to 1½ minutes; then drop in a tea bag or ball of spiced tea and let it steep until the tea is at the desired strength.

○ **Appetizers not suited to the microwave.** Fried appetizers or those encased in a crust or batter, such as turnovers, egg rolls, or puff pastry, are poor microwave candidates. Even if they've been baked or deep-fried, the crust becomes soggy in the microwave.

SPINACH-STUFFED MUSHROOMS

Savory spinach and cheese fill large mushroom caps in this easy yet elegant appetizer. Look for mushrooms at their peak of freshness.

1 package (12 oz.) frozen spinach soufflé
½ teaspoon instant minced onion
2 tablespoons fine dry bread crumbs
¼ cup grated Parmesan cheese
12 mushrooms, 1½ to 2 inches in diameter

Remove spinach soufflé from foil container and place block in a 1-quart casserole. Cover with wax paper. Microwave on **MEDIUM (50%)** for 2 minutes, breaking up with a fork after 1 minute. Let stand for 5 minutes. Stir in onion, bread crumbs, and 3 tablespoons of the cheese; set aside.

Wash mushrooms and pat dry. Gently twist out stems; reserve for other uses. Mound spinach mixture evenly in mushroom caps.

Place two paper towels on a flat 10-inch plate. Arrange mushrooms in a circle on plate. Sprinkle with remaining 1 tablespoon cheese.

Microwave, uncovered, on **HIGH (100%)** for 3 to 4 minutes (rotating dish ¼ turn after 2 minutes, then every minute) or until heated through. Let stand for 3 minutes before serving. Makes 12 appetizers.

HAPPY HOUR MUSHROOMS

Don't let the name of this recipe fool you — these stuffed mushrooms are so good they won't last more than a few minutes.

2 tablespoons butter or margarine, softened
1 tablespoon red or dry white wine
1 large clove garlic, minced or pressed
3 tablespoons shredded jack cheese
1 teaspoon soy sauce
⅓ cup fine dry bread crumbs
12 mushrooms, 1½ to 2 inches in diameter

In a small bowl, combine butter, wine, garlic, cheese, soy, and bread crumbs; blend well, then set aside.

Wash mushrooms and pat dry. Gently twist out stems; reserve for other uses. Mound cheese mixture evenly in mushroom caps and press in lightly. Place two paper towels on a flat 10-inch plate. Arrange mushrooms in a circle on plate.

Microwave, uncovered, on **HIGH (100%)** for 2½ to 3 minutes (rotating plate ¼ turn after 1½ minutes) or until heated through. Let stand for 3 minutes before serving. Makes 12 appetizers.

ARTICHOKE NIBBLES

This zesty blend of chopped artichoke hearts and Cheddar cheese quickly microwaves into elegant hors d'oeuvres of crowd-pleasing quantity. Serve them warm or at room temperature.

2 jars (6 oz. *each*) marinated artichoke hearts
1 small onion, finely chopped
1 clove garlic, minced or pressed
4 eggs
¼ cup fine dry bread crumbs
¼ teaspoon salt
⅛ teaspoon *each* pepper, oregano leaves, and liquid hot pepper seasoning
2 cups (8 oz.) shredded Cheddar cheese
2 tablespoons minced parsley

(Continued on next page)

Drain marinade from 1 jar of artichokes into a 7 by 11-inch baking dish. Drain other jar, reserving marinade for other uses, if desired. Chop artichoke hearts and set aside.

Add onion and garlic to reserved marinade. Cover with wax paper. Microwave on **HIGH (100%)** for 3 minutes (stirring after 2 minutes) or until onion is soft.

In a small bowl, beat eggs lightly. Add bread crumbs, salt, pepper, oregano, and hot pepper seasoning. Stir in cheese, parsley, and artichokes. Pour egg mixture into onion and stir until well blended. Spread mixture evenly in baking dish and cover with wax paper.

Microwave on **HIGH (100%)** for 8 to 10 minutes (rotating dish ¼ turn after 5 minutes) or until set when lightly pressed in center. Let stand, covered, for 10 minutes. Cut into 1-inch squares. Serve warm. Or cool, cover, and refrigerate; bring to room temperature before serving. Makes about 6 dozen appetizers.

MEXICAN BEAN DIP

For spur-of-the-moment entertaining or just a casual family evening, try this chili and tomato-laced bean dip. Tortilla chips and crisp vegetables make good partners.

  1 can (1 lb.) refried beans
  2 cups (8 oz.) shredded Cheddar cheese
  1 can (4 oz.) whole green chili peppers, seeded and diced
  1 medium-size tomato, peeled, seeded, and diced
  ½ to 1 teaspoon chili powder
     Tortilla chips or corn chips
     Carrot sticks, celery sticks, zucchini rounds, and cucumber rounds

In a 1½-quart serving dish or pottery fondue dish, mix together beans, cheese, chili peppers, tomato, and chili powder. Cover with a lid or plastic wrap. Microwave on **MEDIUM (50%)** for 4 to 5 minutes (stirring after 2 minutes) or until heated through. Serve immediately, with chips and crisp vegetables for dipping. Makes about 3 cups.

VEGETABLE MORSELS

Though they may remind you of Middle Eastern falafel, these green and gold vegetable appetizers are made with readily available ingredients.

  1 package (10 oz.) frozen chopped spinach, thawed
  1 package (9 oz.) frozen green beans, thawed
  3 eggs
  1 teaspoon ground cumin
  1½ to 2 teaspoons garlic salt or salt
  ¼ teaspoon pepper
  3 tablespoons *each* sesame seeds, wheat germ, and all-purpose flour
  2 cups shredded carrots
  ½ cup unflavored yogurt

Squeeze out all moisture from spinach and green beans. Chop beans. In a bowl, beat eggs lightly. Add cumin, garlic salt, pepper, sesame seeds, wheat germ, flour, carrots, spinach, and beans; stir until well blended. (Mixture will be very moist.) Shape into 1-inch balls. (At this point you may cover and refrigerate until next day.)

To cook, arrange 12 balls in a circle on a flat 10-inch plate. Microwave, uncovered, on **HIGH (100%)** for 2 minutes (2½ minutes, if refrigerated) or until firm when squeezed. Let stand, covered with wax paper, for 2 minutes before serving. Repeat with remaining balls. Place yogurt in a bowl and offer wooden picks for dipping. Makes about 4½ dozen appetizers.

ZUCCHINI HOT TOTS

Herb and cheese-flavored mayonnaise crowns cooked zucchini chunks. For even cooking, choose zucchini of uniform size.

  3 medium zucchini (*each* about 1½ inches in diameter)
  ⅓ cup mayonnaise
  ¼ cup minced green onions (including tops)
  ½ cup grated Parmesan cheese
     Dash of pepper
  ½ teaspoon oregano leaves
  ⅛ teaspoon garlic powder
     About 3 tablespoons fine dry bread crumbs
     Paprika

Cut zucchini into ¾-inch-thick slices. Place slices in a single layer in a 7 by 11-inch baking dish. Cover with wax paper. Microwave on **HIGH (100%)** for 3 to 4 minutes or until zucchini gives when gently squeezed. If any are still firm, remove cooked slices and microwave remaining zucchini on **HIGH (100%)** for 1 more minute. Transfer to paper towels and let stand until completely cooled.

In a small bowl, combine mayonnaise, onions, cheese, pepper, oregano, and garlic powder; blend well. Spread mayonnaise mixture evenly on each zucchini slice. Dip tops in bread crumbs, then sprinkle with paprika. (At this point you may cover and refrigerate until next day; bring to room temperature before microwaving.)

Arrange half the zucchini slices in a circle on a flat 10-inch plate. Microwave, uncovered, on **HIGH (100%)** for 1½ minutes or until heated through. Repeat with remaining zucchini slices. Let stand, uncovered, for 3 to 5 minutes before serving. Makes about 2 dozen appetizers.

For between-meal snacks or appetizer nibbles when entertaining, try roasting a variety of nuts and seeds to a golden hue in the microwave to bring out their rich, full flavor.

Chestnuts can be ready to peel and enjoy in less than 10 minutes (they take 40 minutes or more in a conventional oven). And, you can roast your own pumpkin seeds, sunflower seeds, and such winter squash seeds as Danish and butternut.

If the nuts and seeds are prepared ahead, cool them completely and store them in airtight containers until needed.

Chestnuts. Slash the shells before roasting to prevent them from exploding when heated. Make crisscross cuts piercing the shells of 1½ to 2 dozen **chestnuts**. Place the nuts in a single layer in a shallow dish. Microwave, uncovered, on **HIGH (100%)** for 2 minutes, turning the nuts over after 1 minute. Stir well and microwave on **HIGH (100%)** for 1 more minute or until the nuts are soft when squeezed.

Let them stand, uncovered, for 5 minutes or until cool enough to peel. Serve them warm. Or cool them completely and store them in airtight containers. To reheat, microwave on **HIGH (100%)** for 30 seconds.

Almonds and pine nuts. Spread ½ cup blanched whole or slivered **almonds** or pine nuts in a single layer in a shallow dish. Microwave, uncovered, on **HIGH (100%)** for 6 to 8 minutes (stirring every 2 minutes) or until the nuts are golden.

Salted peanuts. Spread 1 cup raw **peanuts** (with or without skins) in a single layer in a shallow dish. Microwave, uncovered, on **HIGH (100%)** for 6 to 8 minutes, stirring every 2 minutes. Rub the nuts between your hands to remove their skins, if desired. Drizzle them with 1 teaspoon **salad oil** and sprinkle them lightly with **salt**; stir well.

Microwave, uncovered, on **HIGH (100%)** for 45 seconds to 1 minute (stirring after 30 seconds) or until they're golden.

Salted cashews. Roast 1 cup raw **cashews**, following directions for salted peanuts but increasing the initial cooking time to about 12 minutes.

Pumpkin and winter squash seeds. Rinse the fibers from about 1 cup **pumpkin seeds** or Danish or butternut squash seeds; drain. Sprinkle a light, even coating of **salt** in a shallow dish; arrange the damp seeds in a single layer on the salt. Microwave, uncovered, on **HIGH (100%)** for 6 to 7 minutes (stirring every 2 minutes) or until the seeds are crisp. (If you're roasting a smaller amount of seeds or if the seeds themselves are small, check for doneness after 5 minutes.) Rub the seeds between your fingers to remove excess salt before eating.

Sunflower seeds. Prepare as directed for pumpkin seeds, using 1 cup hulled **sunflower seeds.** Microwave, uncovered, on **HIGH (100%)** for 5 minutes or until the seeds are crisp.

Salted walnuts. To remove the astringent flavor of walnuts, place 1½ cups water in a 1-quart glass measure or deep bowl. Microwave on **HIGH (100%)** until the water boils. Add 1 cup **walnut halves** or pieces. Microwave, uncovered, on **HIGH (100%)** until boiling, then boil for 3 minutes.

Drain the nuts, rinse them under cold running water, and spread them out in a single layer on a paper towel. Let them stand for 15 minutes to dry. Then roast them, following the directions for salted peanuts.

CHILIES-IN-CHEESE FONDUE

For fondue with a Mexican accent, start with canned white sauce and add chili peppers and mellow jack cheese. For dipping, offer Vienna sausages, crisp-fried tortillas, cubes of French bread, and raw vegetables.

    1 can (about 10½ oz.) white sauce
    ½ to 1 can (4 oz.) diced green
      chili peppers
    1 clove garlic, minced or pressed
    3 cups (12 oz.) shredded jack
      cheese
    1 tablespoon white wine or milk

In a 1½-quart casserole or pottery fondue dish, combine white sauce, chili peppers, and garlic; beat with a wire whip. Microwave, uncovered, on **HIGH (100%)** for 2 minutes or until heated through. Beat mixture with a wire whip; continue beating, adding cheese, 1 cup at a time, until mixture is smooth and cheese is melted. Stir in wine until well blended.

Microwave, uncovered, on **HIGH (100%)** for 2 minutes (stirring after 1 minute) or until heated through.

To reheat, microwave, uncovered, on **MEDIUM (50%)** for 1 minute (stirring after 30 seconds) or until heated through. Makes about 2 cups.

PEPPERONI PIZZA ROUNDS

The lightly spiced topping for these bite-size pizzas goes together quickly. Prepare the topping in advance, but don't assemble and cook these hors d'oeuvres until just before serving — they become soggy on standing.

    1 cup (about 4 oz.) finely diced
      pepperoni
    1½ cups (6 oz.) shredded Cheddar
      cheese
    ¼ cup tomato-based chili sauce
      About 36 plain Melba
      toast rounds

In a small bowl, stir together pepperoni, cheese, and chili sauce; blend well. (At this point you may cover and refrigerate for up to a week.)

Arrange 12 toast rounds in a circle on a flat 10 or 12-inch plate. Spoon about 1 teaspoon pepperoni mixture on each toast round. Microwave, uncovered, on **HIGH (100%)** for 1 minute (rotating plate ¼ turn after 30 seconds) or until cheese is melted. Repeat with remaining toast rounds. Makes about 36 appetizers.

CHICKEN LIVER BUNDLES

For a zesty flavor contrast, invite your guests to dip these bacon-wrapped chicken livers in a tangy mustard sauce. Because chicken livers tend to spatter when microwaved, cover them with wax paper to keep your oven clean.

      Mustard sauce (recipe follows)
    ½ pound chicken livers, thawed
      if frozen
    ⅛ teaspoon lemon pepper or
      pepper
    8 or 9 strips thinly sliced bacon

Prepare mustard sauce; cover and refrigerate.

Cut chicken livers into quarters (you should have 16 to 18 pieces). Rinse and drain well on paper towels. Sprinkle with lemon pepper and set aside.

Allow 1 strip bacon for 2 liver pieces. Arrange half the bacon on a nonmetallic rack or on paper towels in a 7 by 11-inch baking dish. Cover with a paper towel. Microwave on **HIGH (100%)** for 2½ to 3 minutes or until limply cooked. Repeat with remaining bacon strips. Cut each strip in half crosswise. Wrap a piece of liver in each bacon piece; secure with a wooden pick. (At this point you may cover and refrigerate until next day.)

To cook, arrange half the liver bundles on a nonmetallic rack in a 7 by 11-inch baking dish. Cover with wax paper. Microwave on **HIGH (100%)** for 2 to 2½ minutes (turning pieces over after 1 minute) or until bacon is crisp and liver is tender but still slightly pink inside. Let stand, covered, for 2 minutes. Repeat with remaining liver bundles.

Pass liver bundles with mustard sauce for dipping. Makes about 1½ dozen appetizers.

Mustard sauce. In a small bowl, stir together ¼ cup prepared **tartar sauce** and 1 tablespoon *each* **Dijon mustard, milk,** and chopped **green onion top.** Makes about ⅓ cup.

SWEET & SOUR FRANKS

Sweet and sour sauce transforms ordinary frankfurters into an exotic, out-of-the-ordinary dish. The sauce's tangy flavor mingles equally well with cooked meatballs. And the sauce won't stick as it might when cooked conventionally.

1½ teaspoons cornstarch
⅓ cup vinegar
¼ cup catsup
½ cup firmly packed brown sugar
1½ teaspoons soy sauce
1 can (8 oz.) pineapple chunks, packed in unsweetened pineapple juice
1 medium-size green pepper, seeded and cut into 1-inch chunks
1 package (1 lb.) all-beef frankfurters, cut diagonally into ½-inch slices (or 1 lb. miniature frankfurters)

In a 1½-quart casserole or pottery fondue dish, mix cornstarch and vinegar until smooth. Stir in catsup, sugar, and soy. Drain pineapple, reserving ¼ cup of the juice. Set fruit aside.

Stir reserved juice into catsup mixture. Microwave, uncovered, on **HIGH (100%)** for 4 minutes, stirring after 2 minutes. Stir in green pepper chunks. Microwave, uncovered, on **HIGH (100%)** for 4 minutes, stirring after 2 minutes.

Stir in reserved pineapple and frankfurters. Microwave, uncovered, on **HIGH (100%)** for 4 more minutes (stirring after 2 minutes) or until frankfurters are heated through. Serve warm, with wooden picks to spear. Makes 4 to 5 dozen appetizers.

TERIYAKI MEATBALLS

You can shape these Japanese-inspired meatballs well in advance of the party. Then, 10 minutes before guests are due to arrive, marinate meat briefly in the teriyaki sauce and microwave in batches.

Teriyaki sauce (recipe follows)
1 pound lean ground beef
¼ cup fine dry bread crumbs
⅓ cup finely chopped green onions
1 egg

Prepare teriyaki sauce. In a bowl, combine beef, bread crumbs, onions, egg, and 3 tablespoons of the teriyaki sauce. Shape into balls about 1 inch in diameter. Arrange them in a single layer on a rimmed baking sheet. (At this point you may cover and refrigerate for up to 8 hours.)

About 10 minutes before serving, pour remaining teriyaki sauce over meatballs and roll to coat evenly.

Lift about 12 meatballs at a time from marinade and arrange in a circle on a flat 10-inch plate. Microwave, uncovered, on **HIGH (100%)** for 3 to 3½ minutes (rotating plate ¼ turn after 1½ minutes) or until meat is done to your liking when slashed. Repeat with remaining meatballs. Makes about 4 dozen appetizers.

Teriyaki sauce. In a small bowl, combine ⅓ cup **soy sauce,** 2 tablespoons each **sugar** and dry **sherry,** ¾ teaspoons grated fresh **ginger** (or ¼ teaspoon ground ginger), ¼ cup finely minced **green onions,** 2 cloves **garlic** (minced or pressed), and ¼ teaspoon **pepper.**

CLAMS WITH GARLIC BUTTER

It's fascinating to watch clams cook in a microwave oven — they pop open in just a few minutes. When they're ready, offer garlic butter for dipping and triangles of French bread to catch the drips.

¼ cup butter or margarine
1 small clove garlic, minced or pressed
1 tablespoon chopped parsley
½ teaspoon lemon juice
1 dozen clams (or mussels) in their shells, well scrubbed

In a small serving bowl, place butter, garlic, parsley, and lemon juice. Microwave, uncovered, on **HIGH (100%)** for 1 minute or until butter is melted; set aside.

Arrange clams in a circle on a flat 10-inch plate. Cover with pleated plastic wrap (page 7). Microwave on **HIGH (100%)** for 3 to 5 minutes or until shells pop open. If any are not yet open, lift out opened clams and microwave remaining clams on **HIGH (100%),** checking at 30-second intervals. Serve in shells with garlic butter. Makes 2 first-course servings.

HOT CRAB DIP

Crunchy with almond slivers, this festive crab dip won't last long after you put it out. Tuck it in the microwave just as your guests are arriving.

1 large package (8 oz.) cream cheese, softened
1 can (about 7 oz.) crabmeat, drained and flaked
2 tablespoons finely chopped green onion (including top)
2 tablespoons milk
1 tablespoon finely chopped parsley
1 tablespoon lemon juice
½ teaspoon Worcestershire
¼ cup slivered or sliced almonds, roasted (page 15)
Melba toast rounds or unsalted crackers

In a shallow 1-quart serving dish, stir together cheese, crabmeat, onion, milk, parsley, lemon juice, and Worcestershire. Cover with plastic wrap. Microwave on **HIGH (100%)** for 4 minutes (stirring after 2 minutes) or until heated through. Sprinkle nuts evenly over top.

To serve, place dish on a warming tray and offer toast rounds for dipping. Makes about 2 cups.

ASPARAGUS VINAIGRETTE

(Pictured on facing page)

Tender asparagus spears, marinated in a piquant dressing, make an elegant first course that you can prepare in advance. Try to purchase thin, young stalks of uniform thickness to ensure even cooking. The red "ribbons" in the photograph on the facing page were made from a whole pimento (you'll need a small can). Cut four long strips, each about ½ inch wide; carefully knot the strips, tucking the ends under spears.

- 2 pounds asparagus
- ¼ cup water
- ¼ cup olive oil or salad oil
- 2 teaspoons dry basil
- ½ teaspoon salt
- ⅛ teaspoon *each* pepper and paprika
- 2 teaspoons Dijon mustard
- ½ teaspoon mustard seeds
- 4 teaspoons white wine vinegar
- 1 teaspoon lemon juice
- ½ cup thinly sliced green onions (including some tops)
- 1 small can whole pimentos (optional)

Snap off tough ends from asparagus. Peel skin with a vegetable peeler, if desired. Place asparagus in a 9 by 13-inch baking dish with buds to center of dish. Sprinkle with water. Cover with pleated plastic wrap (page 7).

Microwave on **HIGH (100%)** for 10 to 13 minutes (bringing center spears to outside of dish after 5 minutes) or until almost fork-tender. Let stand, covered, for 4 to 5 minutes. Drain off liquid and let cool for 20 minutes.

Meanwhile, in a small bowl or jar, combine oil, basil, salt, pepper, paprika, mustard, mustard seeds, vinegar, lemon juice, and onions; beat with a fork until well blended (or cover jar with a lid and shake until blended).

Pour dressing over asparagus. Cover and refrigerate for at least 6 hours, turning spears occasionally. (The longer they marinate, the more tart they will be.) Asparagus may be refrigerated in marinade for up to 5 days.

To serve, arrange spears on a serving platter, spoon some marinade over them, and garnish with pimento, if desired. Makes 8 first-course servings.

BRANDIED MOCHA

Chocolate, coffee, and brandy blend deliciously in this wintertime warmup drink. Decorate each mug with a dollop of whipped cream and a sprinkling of cinnamon, if you like.

- 1 tablespoon instant chocolate-flavored drink mix
- 2 teaspoons instant coffee powder
- 2 teaspoons brandy or ½ teaspoon brandy extract
- ⅔ cup milk
  Whipped cream (optional)
  Ground cinnamon (optional)

In a 6-ounce cup or mug, stir together chocolate mix, coffee powder, brandy, and milk; blend well. Microwave, uncovered, on **HIGH (100%)** for 1 to 1½ minutes or until heated through. If desired, top with whipped cream and sprinkle with cinnamon. Makes 1 serving.

CRANBERRY GLOGG

Garnished with an orange slice and a cinnamon stick for stirring, this hot and spicy drink banishes the chill of a wintry evening. Serve it before dinner or brunch to wake up the appetite, or as a midnight warmup with roasted nuts or seeds (page 15).

- 3 cups cranberry juice cocktail
- ½ cup orange juice
- 2 tablespoons raisins
- 4 teaspoons sugar
- 4 whole cinnamon sticks
- 12 whole cloves
- 4 thin orange slices

In a 2-quart glass measure or mixing bowl, place cranberry juice, orange juice, raisins, sugar, cinnamon sticks, and cloves; stir to blend. Microwave, uncovered, on **HIGH (100%)** for 6 minutes (stirring after 3 minutes) or until heated through. Remove cloves and ladle juice and raisins into 4 mugs. Garnish each mug with an orange slice and a cinnamon stick. Makes 4 servings.

CAFÉ AU LAIT

If you loved it in Paris, you'll love it at home — just use your favorite instant coffee. The microwave method is easy and fast, a blessing for those sleepy mornings.

- 2 teaspoons instant coffee powder or flakes
- ⅔ cup milk
  Sugar (optional)

In a 6-ounce cup or mug, combine coffee powder and milk. Microwave, uncovered, on **HIGH (100%)** for 1½ minutes. Add sugar to taste, if desired. Makes 1 serving.

Bright red ribbons — made from strips of pimento — tie up bundles of marinated asparagus spears. The microwave preserves the rich color and flavor of these tender spears, making an elegant and attractive first course you can prepare ahead. The recipe for Asparagus Vinaigrette is on this page.

Meat, Poultry & Fish

For the harried and hurried cook, a microwave oven can relieve much of that home-from-the-office frenzy or other last-minute turmoil. Of course, you don't have to be in a hurry to appreciate the way meat and poultry cook to tender, juicy perfection — but what a bonus it is that they do so in little more time than it takes to toss a salad and set the table! Even stews that once simmered slowly through an afternoon are ready in about an hour — and seafood practically in the wink of an eye.

In this chapter you'll find a varied and delectable array of entrées, all of them speedy enough for the work week or whenever you're pressed for time. We've also included hot sandwiches and a few recipes for young cooks to try.

TIPS & TECHNIQUES

○ **Even cooking of meat.** For even cooking, select steaks or chops of uniform size and shape. With a roast, try to purchase one that's symmetrical all around. If it tapers at one end, that end will cook faster, probably drying out before the rest of the meat is ready. If you do bring home an asymmetrical roast, shield the last inch of the tapered end with about 1 inch of aluminum foil during the first half of the cooking time; make sure, though, that the foil doesn't touch the oven wall.

When cutting up meat for stew, keep the cubes as uniform in size and shape as possible so they'll cook evenly. Since smaller pieces become tender more quickly than larger ones, we recommend cutting ¾-inch cubes, as we did for Beef Burgundy (page 28).

○ **Meat tenderness.** We suggest cooking times for rare or medium-rare doneness. But since the fat content of meat varies so much, check for doneness at the minimum time given. Let your own preference guide you, but watch out —

meat cooked well-done in a microwave will be tough.

Microwave tender cuts of meat, such as sirloin, tenderloin, or rib sections, on **HIGH (100%)**; they won't need liquid. More economical and less tender cuts (such as the chuck we used for Beef Burgundy on page 28) need liquid and should be cooked on **MEDIUM (50%)** or **MEDIUM-LOW (30%)**. Slower cooking and the added liquid tenderize these cuts by breaking down the tough connective fibers.

○ **Microwaving bacon.** Though we suggest cooking times for bacon on page 22, timing will vary according to the thickness of the slices, their temperature, and the amount of sugar that was added during curing.

Because excessive drippings will cause uneven cooking, it's best not to microwave more than 8 to 10 strips of bacon at a time. If you need a pound or more, cook it conventionally. But for easier separation of the slices, you can begin by microwaving the package of bacon on **HIGH (100%)** for 30 seconds.

○ **Browning meat and poultry.** Since microwave cooking steams food, meat and poultry never become quite so golden-brown and crisp as they do in a conventional oven. But browning does occur when microwave cooking continues uninterrupted for at least 15 minutes — as in One Rib for Two, pictured crisply browned on page 26 (recipe on page 28).

If you want meat or poultry with rich brown color, brush the surface with a mixture of two parts of butter or water to one part of brown gravy sauce, as we did for the Game Hens with Apricots shown on the front cover (recipe on page 38). You can also get good results with a soy sauce or herb butter baste.

Steaks, hamburgers, and chops cook so quickly they don't have time to brown. For these we recommend a browning dish or skillet that simulates the look of conventional broiling.

○ **Keeping meat and poultry out of their juices.** To prevent meat and poultry (except turkey) from stewing in their own juices, place them on a nonmetallic rack inside the baking dish (you can substitute an overturned saucer, but it doesn't work quite as well).

Because fat molecules and liquid attract microwaves, pan juices left in the dish may prevent the meat or poultry from cooking within the allotted time. You'll need to use a bulb baster to remove the juices as they accumulate.

○ **Standing time for meat and poultry.** Like other microwaved foods, meat and poultry require standing time to finish cooking. Always check for doneness after the minimum cooking time given in the recipe (see "Testing the internal temperature of turkey," above right). If you're using a conventional thermometer, it should register 10° to 15° lower than the serving temperature; the difference will be made up during the standing time. If the meat or poultry is underdone, be sure to remove the thermometer before returning the food to the oven.

○ **Microwaving poultry.** Place poultry breast side down for the first part of the cooking time. This allows the juices to trickle down and baste the white meat.

To promote even cooking — and to prevent spattering — cover chicken and game hens with wax paper. You can try covering your turkey, if you wish, but since most turkeys are so large, the paper could touch the oven wall or ceiling and obstruct the stirrer fan opening.

Turkeys are too large to place on a rack and, because of their size, need to be turned frequently (see page 25) for even cooking.

○ **Testing the internal temperature of turkey.** Those pop-up indicators that work (most of the time) in conventional ovens do not work in a microwave oven. Instead, use a regular mercury thermometer inserted into the inner thigh (without touching the bone) to test for doneness — *but only after taking the turkey out of the oven.* The thermometer would cause arcing, resulting in a pitted oven and damage to your magnetron tube.

An alternative is to buy an oven-safe microwave thermometer. Some ovens come with a special probe that allows you to program the internal temperature of turkey; in this case, the temperature comes as a read-out on your micro-wave, and you won't need a separate thermometer.

○ **Microwaving fish.** A microwave natural and a dieter's delight, fish is especially convenient because it cooks very quickly. And there's no need to use fat.

The secret of proper cooking is to watch closely — fish overcooks in seconds. As a rule, allow 3 or 4 minutes per pound, and remove the fish from the oven when it's barely done. Let it stand, covered, and then check for doneness. The flesh should be opaque and should flake easily when prodded with a fork in the thickest part. Overcooked fish becomes rubbery and dry, with loss of its delicate flavor.

○ **Defrosting a pound of fish.** Place a 1-pound package of frozen fish on the floor of the microwave. Microwave on **HIGH (100%)** for 2 to 3 minutes. Let the fish stand in its package for about 10 minutes to complete thawing. Do not try to cook it until it's completely defrosted, or the edges will be cooked and the center still cold.

MEAT, FISH & POULTRY COOKING CHARTS

Caution: To prevent overcooking, use shortest cooking time. Allow food to stand for recommended time. On standing, internal temperature of meat and poultry will rise 10 to 15°; fish will also continue to cook. If necessary, microwave longer, checking for doneness at 1-minute intervals.

Meat	Amount	Preparation	Cooking Time (CT) Standing Time (ST)
Beef roast, boneless (sirloin tip, rolled rib, cross rib)	3½–4 lbs.	Place roast, fat side down, on a nonmetallic rack in a 7 by 11-inch baking dish.	**CT:** 9–11 minutes per lb. for rare 10–13 minutes per lb. for medium Determine total cooking time. Microwave on **HIGH (100%)** for 5 minutes, then on **MEDIUM (50%)** for remaining time, rotating dish ¼ turn every 10 minutes. Turn roast over halfway through cooking and baste with juices. Meat thermometer or probe inserted in center of roast should register 125° for rare, 135° for medium. **ST:** 10–15 minutes, covered with foil.
Ground beef patties	¼ lb. each	Season to taste with salt, pepper, Worcestershire, finely chopped onion. Shape into patties about ¾ inch thick. To add color, if desired, brush patties with a mixture of 2 tablespoons water and 2 tablespoons bottled brown gravy sauce.	**CT:** Microwave a browning skillet or dish on **HIGH (100%)** for **4** minutes. Carefully remove skillet from oven and place on a heatproof surface. Add patties to dish, turning over after 1 minute to brown other side. For medium doneness, microwave uncovered, on **HIGH (100%).** 1 patty 2–3 minutes 2 patties 3–4 minutes 3 patties 4–4½ minutes 4 patties 4½–5 minutes **ST:** 1 minute, uncovered; juices should run clear when slashed.
Pork loin roast, bone-in or boneless	3½–4 lbs.	Place roast, fat side down, on a nonmetallic rack in a 7 by 11-inch baking dish.	**CT:** 14–16 minutes per lb. Microwave, uncovered, on **MEDIUM-HIGH (70%)** rotating dish ½ turn every 10 minutes. Turn roast over halfway through cooking and baste with pan juices. Meat thermometer or probe inserted in thickest portion (without touching bone) should register 160°. **ST:** 10–15 minutes, loosely covered with foil.
Spareribs, country-style	3 lbs.	In a 7 by 11-inch baking dish, arrange ribs with meaty portions to outside of dish. Top with onion slices, if desired. Pour in ¼ cup water. Cover with plastic wrap.	**CT:** 18–20 minutes per lb. Determine total cooking time. Microwave, covered, on **HIGH (100%)** for 10 minutes. Pour off juices and turn ribs over. Microwave on **MEDIUM (50%)** for remaining time, discarding accumulated juices and bringing cooked portion to inside of dish halfway through cooking. If desired, uncover and baste with Tangy Barbecue Sauce (page 91) during last 10 minutes. **ST:** 5 minutes, covered (uncovered, if basted). Meat in thickest portion should no longer be pink when slashed.
Spareribs, one medium-size side	2½–3 lbs.	Cut ribs into 2 rib pieces. In an 8 by 12 or 9 by 13-inch baking dish, arrange ribs, with meaty portions toward outside of dish. Thinner portions may overlap. Pour in ¼ cup water. Cover with plastic wrap.	**CT:** 13–16 minutes per lb. Determine total cooking time. Microwave on **HIGH (100%)** for 7 minutes. Pour off liquid and turn ribs over. Microwave on **MEDIUM (50%)** for remaining time, discarding accumulated juices and bringing cooked portion to inside of dish every 7 minutes. If desired, uncover, and baste with Tangy Barbecue Sauce (page 91) during last 10 minutes. **ST:** 5 minutes, covered (uncovered, if basted). Meat in thickest portion should no longer be pink when slashed.
Bacon	1–8 strips (For even cooking, we recommend microwaving no more than 8 strips at a time.)	Arrange bacon strips in a single layer on a nonmetallic rack or on 2 thicknesses of paper towels in a 7 by 11-inch baking dish. Cover with a paper towel and top with another layer of bacon, if desired. Cover with paper towel.	**CT:** About 1 minute per strip. Microwave on **HIGH (100%).** Cooking time varies depending on thickness, starting temperature, curing process, amount of fat, and crispness desired. If towels absorb a lot of fat and bacon is not cooked, replace bottom towels with fresh ones. **ST:** 2–3 minutes, covered. Bacon should be browned and crisp.
Leg of lamb, shank half	5–5½ lbs.	If desired, sliver 1 or 2 cloves garlic and insert into a few small slashes in flesh. Place leg, fat side down, on a nonmetallic rack in an 8 by 12 or 9 by 13-inch baking dish. Shield shank end with a 2-inch strip of foil.	**CT:** 8½–10 minutes per lb. for medium 10–12 minutes per lb. for well done. Determine total cooking time. Microwave on **HIGH (100%)** for 5 minutes. Microwave on **MEDIUM (50%)** for remaining time, turning meat over and rotating dish ¼ turn every 10 minutes. Remove foil shield halfway through cooking and baste with pan juices. Meat thermometer or probe inserted in thickest portion (without touching bone) should register 135° for medium, 150° for well done. **ST:** 15 minutes, covered with foil.
Leg of veal, boned and tied	4 lbs.	If desired, rub meat with garlic powder, paprika, and pepper. Place roast, fat side down, on a nonmetallic rack in a 7 by 11-inch baking dish.	**CT:** 10 minutes per lb. Determine total cooking time. Microwave on **HIGH (100%),** rotating dish ¼ turn every 10 minutes. Turn roast over halfway through cooking and baste with pan juices. Meat thermometer or probe inserted into thickest portion should register 155°. **ST:** 10 minutes, covered loosely with foil.

(Continued on page 24)

One standing beef rib (recipe on page 28) is the perfect entrée for two, accompanied by Fluffy Horseradish Sauce (page 91) and a green salad.

Fish	Amount	Preparation	Cooking Time (CT) Standing Time (ST)
Fish steaks or fillets Red snapper or other rockfish, Greenland turbot, sole, halibut, sea bass, salmon, ½ to ¾ inch thick	1 lb.	If frozen, thaw completely. Rinse and pat dry. In a greased 7 by 11-inch baking dish, arrange fish in an even layer with meaty portions to outside of dish. Brush with melted butter or margarine. If desired, season with paprika, dill weed, grated lemon peel, or lemon juice. Cover with plastic wrap.	CT: 3–5 minutes per lb. Microwave on **HIGH (100%)**, turning fish over after 2 minutes. Fish should flake readily when prodded in thickest portion with a fork. ST: 3 minutes, covered.
Trout, whole (cleaned and dressed)	1 or 2 (8–10 oz. each)	If frozen, thaw completely. Rinse and pat dry. Stuff with lemon or onion slices, if desired. In a greased 7 by 11-inch baking dish, arrange fish, lengthwise, with backbone to outside edge of dish. Brush with melted butter or margarine. Cover with plastic wrap.	CT: 1 trout 2½–3½ minutes 2 trout 5–7 minutes Microwave on **HIGH (100%)**, turning fish over and bringing cooked portion to inside of dish halfway through cooking. Fish should flake readily when prodded in thickest portion with a fork. ST: 3 minutes, covered.
Clams in the shell	1 dozen	Scrub well. On a 10-inch glass pie plate, arrange clams in a circle, hinge side to outside edge of plate. Cover with pleated plastic wrap (page 7).	CT: 3–4 minutes Microwave on **HIGH (100%)** until shells pop open. Lift out opened clams; continue cooking remaining clams, checking at 30-second intervals. ST: 1 minute, covered.
Crab in the shell (cleaned, cooked, and cracked)	1 large (about 2 lbs.)	In a 7 by 11-inch baking dish, arrange crab pieces with meaty portions to outside of dish. Brush with melted buter or margarine. Cover with plastic wrap.	CT: 2–3 minutes Microwave on **HIGH (100%)**. Meat in shells should be heated through. ST: 1–2 minutes, covered.
Lobster tails	8–9 oz. each	If frozen, thaw completely. Use scissors to cut off soft under-shell and fins along outer edges; discard. Bend shell back, cracking some joints to prevent curling. With your fingers, start at thickest end and pull meat free in 1 piece. Place meat, rounded side up, in a 7 by 11-inch baking dish. Brush with melted butter or margarine and drizzle with lemon juice. Cover with plastic wrap.	CT: 2 tails 5–6 minutes 4 tails 9–11 minutes Microwave on **HIGH (100%)**, turning meat over and basting generously with melted butter halfway through cooking. Meat should be tender and opaque throughout when slashed. ST: 3–5 minutes, covered.
Mussels in the shell	1 dozen	Scrub well. On a 10-inch glass pie plate or serving plate, arrange mussels in a circle, hinge side to outside edge of plate. Cover with pleated plastic wrap (page 7).	CT: 3–4 minutes Microwave on **HIGH (100%)** until shells pop open. Mussels should turn bright orange. ST: 1 minute, covered.
Oysters in the shell Eastern Pacific, medium-size	 10–12 8	Same as mussels in the shell.	CT: 4–5 minutes Microwave on **HIGH (100%)** until shells pop open. Edges of oysters should be curled. ST: 2 minutes, covered.
Oysters, shucked Eastern Pacific, small	 8–10 1 jar (10 oz.)	On a 10-inch glass pie plate or serving plate, arrange oysters in a circle. Drizzle with their juices and melted butter or margarine. Cover with plastic wrap.	CT: 4–5 minutes Microwave on **HIGH (100%)**, turning over after 2 minutes. Oysters should be heated through and edges curled. ST: 1–2 minutes, covered.
Scallops	1 lb.	Rinse well; if large, cut in half. Place in a 1½-quart casserole. Drizzle with melted butter or margarine and dry white wine or lemon juice. Cover with a lid or plastic wrap.	CT: 2½–3½ minutes Microwave on **HIGH (100%)**, stirring after 1½ minutes. Meat should be tender and opaque throughout when slashed. ST: 2–3 minutes, covered.
Shrimp, medium-size (30 to 32 per lb.)	1 lb.	Rinse well. Shell and devein, if desired. On a flat 12-inch plate, arrange shrimp in a single layer with meaty portion to outside edge of plate. Cover with plastic wrap.	CT: 4–5 minutes Microwave on **HIGH (100%)**, bringing cooked portion to inside of plate after 2 minutes. Shrimp should be pink and meat tender and opaque throughout when slashed. ST: 3–5 minutes, covered.

Poultry	Amount	Preparation	Cooking Time (CT) Standing Time (ST)
Turkey, whole	10–14 lbs. (We do not recommend microwaving a bird over 14 lbs.)	If frozen, thaw completely according to directions on wrapper. Remove giblets and neck; rinse inside and out, pat dry. Stuff breast and body cavities, if desired. Secure neck skin to back with skewer. If stuffed, hold stuffing in body cavity with heel of bread. With string tie legs together and wings to breast. Rub skin with butter or margarine and paprika. Place bird, breast side down, in a 9 by 13-inch baking dish.	CT: 7–8 minutes per lb. Microwave on **HIGH (100%)**. Determine total cooking time; divide into 4 equal cooking periods. Position bird as follows: first period, breast down; second period, right wing down; third period, left wing down; fourth period, breast up. Discard accumulated juices each time bird is turned. A meat thermometer or probe inserted into inner thigh (without touching bone) should register 170°. ST: 15 minutes, loosely covered with foil.
Turkey breast, half	3–3½ lbs.	Remove bone and skin, if desired. Place in a 7 by 11-inch baking dish. Cover with plastic wrap.	CT: 4–5 minutes per lb. Microwave on **HIGH (100%)**, turning over halfway through cooking. ST: 5–7 minutes, covered, juices should run clear when meat in thickest portion is slashed.
Turkey drumsticks	1–1¼ lbs. each	Rinse; pat dry. In a 7 by 11-inch baking dish, arrange turkey legs with meaty portions to outside of dish. Brush with melted butter or margarine. Cover with plastic wrap.	CT: 20 minutes per lb. Determine total cooking time. Microwave on **HIGH (100%)** for 10 minutes. Turn legs over; microwave on **MEDIUM-LOW (30%)** for remaining time, turning legs over halfway through cooking. Discard juices as they accumulate in dish. ST: 15 minutes, covered. Meat near thigh bone should no longer be pink when slashed.
Broiler-fryer chicken, whole	3–3½ lbs.	If frozen, thaw completely. Remove giblets and neck, rinse inside and out, and pat dry. Stuff, if desired. Rub skin with butter or margarine and paprika or a mixture of 2 tablespoons water and 2 tablespoons bottled brown gravy sauce. Place, breast side down, on a nonmetallic rack in a 7 by 11-inch baking dish. Cover with wax paper.	CT: 6–7 minutes per lb. Microwave on **HIGH (100%)**. Turn breast up halfway through cooking. ST: 5 minutes, loosely covered with wax paper, juices should run clear and meat near thigh bone should no longer be pink when slashed.
Broiler-fryer chicken, cut-up	3–3½ lbs.	Rinse; pat dry. In a 7 by 11-inch baking dish, arrange pieces, skin side down, with meaty portions to outside of dish. Cover with wax paper.	CT: 6–7 minutes per lb. Microwave on **HIGH (100%)**, turning pieces skin side up halfway through cooking. If desired, uncover, discard accumulated liquid, and baste with Tangy Barbecue Sauce (page 91) during last 10 minutes. ST: 5 minutes, covered (uncovered, if basted). Juices should run clear and meat near thigh bone should no longer be pink when slashed.
Chicken breast, split	1–1¼ lbs.	Remove bone and skin, if desired. Place in a 9-inch square baking dish. Cover with wax paper.	CT: 4–5 minutes per lb. Microwave on **HIGH (100%)**, turning over halfway through cooking. ST: 5 minutes, covered. Juices should run clear when meat in thickest portion is slashed.
Chicken legs, thighs attached	6–8 oz. each	Rinse; pat dry. In a 7 by 11-inch baking dish, arrange pieces, skin side down, with thighs to outside of dish and drumstick ends to center. Cover with wax paper.	CT: 7 minutes per lb. Microwave on **HIGH (100%)**, turning over halfway through cooking. ST: 5 minutes, covered. Juices should run clear and meat near thigh bone should no longer be pink when slashed.
Rock Cornish game hens	1¼–1½ lbs. each	Same as whole chicken, except leave legs free; secure wings akimbo-style. Place, breast side down, on nonmetallic rack in a 7 by 11-inch baking dish. Cover with wax paper.	CT: 6 minutes per lb. Microwave on **HIGH (100%)**, turning breast up halfway through cooking. ST: 5 minutes, loosely covered with foil. Juices should run clear and meat near thigh bone should no longer be pink when slashed.
Duckling	4½–5 lbs.	Same as whole turkey, except leave legs free; secure wings akimbo-style. With a fork, prick skin in several places.	CT: 8–9 minutes per lb. Microwave on **HIGH (100%)**, turning breast up halfway through cooking. Discard juices as they accumulate in dish. ST: 5–10 minutes, loosely covered with foil. Juices should run clear and meat near thigh bone should no longer be pink when slashed.

GLAZED MEAT LOAF

Coated with a sweet and spicy glaze, this moist meat loaf is as handsome to behold as it is delicious to eat.

- ⅔ cup quick-cooking rolled oats
- 1 cup milk
- 1 teaspoon salt
- ¼ teaspoon *each* pepper and poultry seasoning
- 2 eggs
- 1 teaspoon Worcestershire
- 1 large onion, finely chopped
- 1½ pounds lean ground beef
- ⅓ cup tomato-based chili sauce or catsup
- 1½ tablespoons brown sugar
- 1 teaspoon Dijon mustard
- ⅛ teaspoon ground nutmeg

In a large bowl, stir together oats, milk, salt, pepper, poultry seasoning, eggs, Worcestershire, and onion. Add beef and combine thoroughly. Pat mixture into a 5 by 9-inch glass or ceramic loaf dish.

In a small bowl, stir together chili sauce, sugar, mustard, and nutmeg. Spread evenly over meat mixture.

Microwave, uncovered, on **HIGH (100%)** for 18 to 20 minutes (rotating dish ¼ turn every 4 minutes) or until no longer pink in center when slashed. Let stand, covered with wax paper, for 5 minutes. With two wide spatulas, carefully lift out and place on a serving platter. Makes 4 to 6 servings.

Super Nachos Dinner (recipe on this page) combines all the zesty flavors of Mexican cuisine in one colorful and delightfully informal entree. You won't even need forks—simply use the crisply fried tortilla pieces to scoop up delicious bites of the bean, meat, cheese, and avocado feast.

ITALIAN MEATBALLS

Tender, moist meatballs with a zesty Italian flavor microwave to perfection in just 10 minutes. Store-bought spaghetti sauce simplifies the preparation of this traditional spaghetti and meatball entrée.

- 1 pound lean ground beef
- ½ cup soft bread crumbs
- 1 egg, lightly beaten
- ¼ cup finely chopped onion
- ½ teaspoon salt
- ¼ teaspoon *each* dry basil and oregano and thyme leaves
- ⅛ teaspoon pepper
- ⅓ cup grated Parmesan cheese
- 1 jar (about 15 oz.) spaghetti sauce
  Cooked spaghetti or noodles
  Grated Parmesan cheese

In a large bowl, combine beef, bread crumbs, egg, onion, salt, basil, oregano, thyme, pepper, the ⅓ cup cheese, and ¼ cup of the spaghetti sauce; blend well. Shape mixture into sixteen 1½-inch meatballs.

In a 10-inch glass or ceramic pie plate, place 4 meatballs in center and arrange remaining 12 meatballs around outer rim. Cover with wax paper. Microwave on **HIGH (100%)** for 4 minutes. Reposition meatballs, moving four in center to outside and four from outside to center. Drain off fat. Cover with wax paper.

Microwave on **HIGH (100%)** for 3 minutes or until meatballs are no longer pink when slashed. Drain off fat. Pour remaining spaghetti sauce over meatballs. Microwave, uncovered, on **HIGH (100%)** for 3 minutes or until sauce is heated through.

Serve meatballs over spaghetti. At the table, pass cheese to spoon over each serving. Makes 4 to 6 servings.

SUPER NACHOS DINNER

(Pictured on facing page)

Delight your guests with this colorful and festive nachos dinner — a great mound of meat, refried beans, chili peppers, and cheese, topped with several delicious garnishes. Though the result looks elaborate, the preparation is simple.

- ½ pound *each* lean ground beef and chorizo sausage (or use 1 lb. beef and omit sausage)
- 1 large onion, chopped
  Salt and pepper
  Liquid hot pepper seasoning
- 1 can (about 1 lb.) refried beans
- 1 tablespoon canned diced green chili pepper
- 1 cup (4 oz.) shredded Cheddar cheese
  Prepared taco sauce (green or red)
- 1 can (7¾ oz.) frozen avocado dip, thawed, or 1 medium-size avocado, peeled, pitted, and coarsely mashed with 1 teaspoon lemon juice
  Sour cream
  Chopped green onions
  Pitted ripe olives
  Green or red chili peppers
- 8 cups fried tortilla pieces or corn-flavored chips

Crumble beef into a 1½-quart casserole. Remove casings from sausage, cut into small pieces, and add to beef. Cover with a lid or wax paper. Microwave on **HIGH (100%)** for 2 minutes. Drain off fat. Add large chopped onion and stir, bringing cooked meat to inside of casserole.

Microwave, covered, on **HIGH (100%)** for 3 minutes; drain off fat and sprinkle to taste with salt, pepper, and hot pepper seasoning.

Spread out beans on a rimmed 10-inch plate. Top with meat mixture. Sprinkle with diced chili pepper and cheese. Microwave, uncovered, on

MEDIUM (50%) for 4 to 5 minutes or until heated through.

Drizzle with taco sauce. Top with avocado, sour cream, green onions, olives, and chili peppers. Tuck some tortilla pieces around edges of bean mixture to make a petaled flower effect. Place remaining tortilla pieces in a basket to pass at the table. Serve immediately.

Scoop up with tortilla pieces; keep platter hot on an electric warming tray, if desired. Makes 4 to 6 servings.

AVOCADO BEEF PATTIES

Mashed avocado, chili peppers, and onions enliven these moist, lightly spiced hamburgers. They look pan-fried when cooked in a browning skillet.

- 1 medium-size avocado
  Lemon juice
- 2 tablespoons diced green chili peppers
- 1 egg, lightly beaten
- 2 teaspoons chopped green onion
- 1½ teaspoons lemon juice
- 1 clove garlic, minced or pressed
- ½ teaspoon salt
- 1 pound lean ground beef
- ½ cup shredded jack cheese
- 4 hamburger buns, split and toasted
  Butter lettuce leaves
- 4 thin slices tomato

Halve avocado lengthwise and remove pit; then peel. Slice half the avocado and coat pieces with lemon juice; set aside.

In a bowl, mash remaining avocado half. Stir in chili peppers, egg, onion, the 1½ teaspoons lemon juice, garlic, and salt. Add beef and combine thoroughly (mixture will be moist). With your hands, shape

meat into 4 patties, each about ¾ inch thick.

Microwave a 10-inch browning dish or skillet on **HIGH (100%)** for 4½ minutes. Carefully remove dish (the bottom is very hot) to a heatproof surface. Place patties in dish. Microwave, uncovered, on **HIGH (100%)** for 3 minutes. Drain off fat.

Turn patties over. Microwave, uncovered, on **HIGH (100%)** for 2 minutes or until juices run clear when patty is slashed. Sprinkle each patty with 2 tablespoons of the cheese. Cover with wax paper and let stand for 5 minutes.

Arrange patties on bottoms of buns and top each patty with lettuce leaves, tomato slice, and a few avocado slices. Cover with remaining buns. Makes 4 servings.

ONE RIB FOR TWO

(Pictured on page 23)

With just one standing beef rib in the freezer, you can produce dinner for two in just under an hour. Two large potatoes do "book end" duty in the microwave, then help round out the meal. For an elegant flourish, whip up Fluffy Horseradish Sauce (page 91).

Another day, if you have any leftovers, set out a cold meat

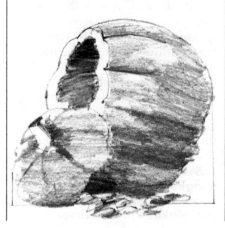

and cheese platter or make hot roast beef sandwiches.

- 1 tablespoon salad oil
- 1 clove garlic, minced or pressed
- 1 frozen rib (about 2½ lbs.) from a standing rib roast
- 2 large russet potatoes

In a small cup, stir together oil and garlic; brush mixture evenly over cut sides of frozen meat. In a 9 by 13-inch baking dish, stand rib upright, fat side down, and place a potato on each side to support roast.

Microwave, uncovered, on **HIGH (100%)** for 12 minutes. Cover very loosely with foil; let stand for 10 minutes. Turn roast fat side up and turn potatoes over. Microwave, uncovered, on **HIGH (100%)** for 12 more minutes. Cover very loosely with foil; let stand for 10 minutes.

Microwave, uncovered, on **HIGH (100%)** for 12 more minutes. Squeeze potatoes — when done, they give readily under pressure; remove and wrap in foil. Place a meat thermometer through fat layer into center of roast. Cover very loosely with foil; let stand for 10 minutes. Meat thermometer should read 135° to 140° for rare, 145° to 150° for medium doneness. (We do *not* recommend roasting until well done — meat becomes tough.) If meat is not done to your liking, remove meat thermometer and microwave, uncovered, on **HIGH (100%)**, checking every 2 minutes, until meat is done to your liking when slashed. Potatoes should be fork-tender. Makes 2 servings.

BEEF BURGUNDY

Generally a good market buy, beef chuck becomes a noteworthy dinner entrée when simmered with mushrooms and small white onions in a flavorful wine sauce.

(Continued on next page)

2 pounds boneless beef chuck
1½ teaspoons paprika
1 beef bouillon cube dissolved in ½ cup hot water
½ cup dry red wine
1 medium-size onion, chopped
1 clove garlic, minced or pressed
1 bay leaf
½ teaspoon thyme leaves
¼ teaspoon pepper
½ pound mushrooms, sliced
1 can (16 oz.) small whole onions, drained well
Salt
2½ tablespoons *each* cornstarch and water
Chopped parsley

Trim excess fat from beef, then cut into ¾-inch cubes. Place meat in a 3-quart casserole; sprinkle with paprika. Pour bouillon and wine over meat along with chopped onion, garlic, bay leaf, thyme, and pepper. Cover with a lid or plastic wrap.

Microwave on **HIGH (100%)** for 5 minutes; stir well. Microwave, covered, on **MEDIUM (50%)** for 30 minutes, stirring after 15 minutes. Stir in mushrooms. Microwave, covered, on **MEDIUM (50%)** for 30 more minutes (stirring after 15 minutes) or until meat is fork-tender.

Remove bay leaf. Stir in whole onions and sprinkle with salt to taste. Stir together cornstarch and water, then stir into beef. Microwave, uncovered, on **HIGH (100%)** for 3 to 4 minutes (stirring after 2 minutes) or until sauce is bubbly and thickened. Let stand, covered, for 10 minutes. Before serving, sprinkle with parsley. Makes 6 servings.

BEEF & BEAN ENCHILADAS

You can prepare these enchiladas up to a day ahead, then simply reheat and serve them with separate bowls of sour cream and chili salsa. We soften the tortillas quickly in the microwave, for easier rolling and to eliminate both the calories and the nuisance of heating them in oil.

1 pound lean ground beef
1 small onion, chopped
1 can (8 oz.) refried beans
½ teaspoon salt
⅛ teaspoon garlic powder
2½ tablespoons prepared red taco sauce
1 can (2¼ oz.) sliced ripe olives, drained well
2 cans (10 oz. *each*) enchilada sauce
8 corn tortillas
1½ cups (6 oz.) shredded Cheddar cheese
Sour cream
Green chili salsa

Crumble beef into a 1½-quart casserole. Cover with a lid or wax paper and microwave on **HIGH (100%)** for 2 minutes. Drain off fat.

Add onion and stir to bring cooked meat to inside of casserole. Microwave, covered, on **HIGH (100%)** for 3 minutes; drain off fat. Stir in beans, salt, garlic powder, taco sauce, and ⅓ cup of the olives; blend well and set aside.

Pour 1 can of enchilada sauce into a 7 by 11-inch baking dish; set aside.

Wrap tortillas in paper towels. Microwave on **HIGH (100%)** for 1 minute.

To assemble enchiladas, place about 3 tablespoons of the beef mixture down center of each tortilla. Top with 2 tablespoons of the cheese. Roll to enclose. Arrange, seam side down, in sauce in baking dish. Pour remaining can of enchilada sauce evenly over tortillas. Cover loosely with plastic wrap. (At this point you may refrigerate until next day.)

Microwave, covered, on **HIGH (100%)** for 12 to 15 minutes (rotating dish ¼ turn after 6 minutes) or until heated through and bubbly. (If refrigerated, microwave, covered, on **MEDIUM (50%)** for 6 minutes, then proceed with above cooking directions.)

Sprinkle with remaining ½ cup cheese and let stand, covered, for 5 minutes before serving. Garnish with remaining olives. At the table, pass bowls of sour cream and chili salsa to spoon over each serving. Makes 8 enchiladas (4 to 8 servings).

SWEETBREADS IN BRANDY CREAM

Sweetbreads, a house specialty in many fine restaurants, is an equally elegant choice for brunch or dinner at home.

Sweetbreads must first be poached and the tough membrane removed before they can be served, but this initial step can be done a day ahead. The deftly seasoned sauce goes together quickly.

About 1¼ pounds fresh or frozen sweetbreads
Water (for soaking)
½ cup water
1 tablespoon lemon juice
½ teaspoon salt
4 tablespoons butter or margarine
¾ pound mushrooms, sliced
½ cup sliced carrot
1 medium-size onion, chopped
2 beef bouillon cubes dissolved in 1 cup hot water
2 tablespoons currant jelly
½ teaspoon dry rosemary
¼ cup *each* whipping cream and brandy
Salt and pepper
Hot buttered toast

Soak fresh sweetbreads for 1 hour in cold water to cover; soak frozen sweetbreads until thawed. Drain well. Place in a 3-quart casserole. Add the ½ cup water, lemon juice, and the ½ teaspoon salt. Cover with a lid or plastic wrap. Microwave on **HIGH (100%)** for 10 to 12 minutes or until sweetbreads are firm and no longer pink throughout. Let stand, covered, for 10 minutes; drain well.

With your fingers, remove membrane and tubes from sweetbreads and discard. Separate sweetbreads into small clusters. (At this point you may cover and refrigerate until next day.)

Place 2 tablespoons of the butter in a 7 by 11-inch baking dish. Microwave, uncovered, on **HIGH (100%)** for 1 minute. Stir in mushrooms. Microwave, uncovered, on **HIGH (100%)** for 3 minutes, stirring after 2 minutes. Lift out mushrooms and set aside.

Add remaining 2 tablespoons butter to dish along with carrot and onion. Cover with plastic wrap. Microwave on **HIGH (100%)** for 3 minutes, stirring after 2 minutes. Pour bouillon over vegetable mixture. Microwave, covered, on **HIGH (100%)** for 12 to 14 minutes (stirring after 6 minutes) or until vegetables are very tender when pierced.

Add jelly and rosemary and stir until jelly is melted. Pour vegetable mixture into a blender or food processor and whirl until smooth. Return to baking dish. Stir in sweetbreads, mushrooms, cream, brandy, and salt and pepper to taste. Cover with plastic wrap. Microwave on **MEDIUM-HIGH (70%)** for 3 to 4 minutes (on **MEDIUM** for about 6 minutes), or until heated through. Spoon over buttered toast. Makes 4 to 6 servings.

LIVER OLÉ

Taco sauce and cheese transform this quick and easy liver entrée into a Mexican specialty.

1 pound baby beef liver (sliced about ¼ inch thick)
1 tablespoon salad oil
3 to 4 tablespoons prepared taco sauce
4 to 5 ounces sliced jack cheese

Remove membrane from liver and cut into serving-size pieces.

Microwave a browning dish or skillet on **HIGH (100%)** for 4½ minutes. Carefully remove dish (the bottom is very hot) to a heatproof surface. Add oil and tilt dish to coat bottom evenly. Spread out liver pieces in dish in a single layer. Let brown for about 30 seconds on each side.

Microwave, uncovered, on **HIGH (100%)** for 30 seconds. Turn pieces over and bring cooked pieces to inside of dish; push uncooked pieces to outside. Microwave, uncovered, for 30 more seconds. Drain off juices. Bring thick, uncooked pieces to outside of dish. Spoon taco sauce over liver and sprinkle evenly with cheese.

Microwave, uncovered, on **HIGH (100%)** for 2 to 2½ minutes or until cheese is melted and liver is done to your liking. Liver should be slightly pink inside; if overcooked it becomes tough. Let stand for 3 minutes before serving. Makes 3 or 4 servings.

PORK LOIN WITH PLUM SAUCE

The same sauce that gives our roast Chicken with Plum Sauce (page 37) its distinctive eye and taste appeal is equally delicious with pork. You can make the generous sauce recipe once and use it for both chicken and pork — refrigerated, it keeps well for 3 to 4 weeks.

For more even cooking, select a roast of uniform proportions. Small, tapered ends will overcook before the center is done.

Plum sauce (page 37)
3½ to 4-pound bone-in pork loin, with back bone cracked between ribs for easy carving

Prepare plum sauce and set 1 cup aside. Cover and refrigerate remaining sauce.

Place roast, fat side down, on a nonmetallic rack in a 7 by 11-inch baking dish. Microwave, uncovered, on **MEDIUM-HIGH (70%)** for 30 minutes, brushing generously with plum sauce after 15 minutes.

Turn roast fat side up. Microwave, uncovered, on **MEDIUM-HIGH (70%)** for 30 minutes, brushing generously with plum sauce after 15 minutes.

When done, a meat thermometer or probe inserted in thickest portion (without touching bone) should register 160°. If below 160°, microwave, uncovered, on **MEDIUM-HIGH (70%)** for 10 to 15 more minutes, checking for doneness at 5-minute intervals.

Transfer roast to a serving platter, cover loosely with foil, and let stand for 10 to 15 minutes or until a meat thermometer registers 170°.

Skim fat from drippings; stir remaining plum sauce into drippings. Microwave, uncovered, on **HIGH (100%)** for 1 to 2 minutes or until heated through. Pass sauce in a separate bowl. Makes 6 to 8 servings.

In a marriage of two different cooking traditions, Middle Eastern pocket bread is stuffed with a robust and spicy filling from Northern Europe: kielbasa sausage and sauerkraut, enlivened with onions, apple chunks, mustard, and sweet pickle relish. The recipe for Sausage & Sauerkraut Pockets is on page 33.

EXTRA STRONG

The blending and producing
of genuine Dijon Extra
Strong Mustard is
ancient and diffic
art. The Pom
family, whose
cestors in
received the
inal and still
recipe fro

ORANGE-GLAZED HAM

A simple glaze contributes sophisticated flavor to canned ham.

For canned hams weighing more than 1½ pounds but less than 5 pounds, use a 7 by 11-inch baking dish; double the glaze recipe and allow 6 minutes cooking time per pound. For hams over 5 pounds, triple the glaze recipe and allow 7 minutes cooking time per pound.

⅓ cup orange marmalade
1½ tablespoons Dijon mustard
⅛ teaspoon ground cloves
1 can (1½ lb.) fully cooked ham

In a small bowl, stir together marmalade, mustard, and cloves. Remove ham from can and place in an 8-inch square baking dish; brush half the marmalade mixture evenly over top and sides. Cover with wax paper. Microwave on **HIGH (100%)** for 4 minutes. Turn ham over and brush with more marmalade mixture.

Microwave, uncovered, on **HIGH (100%)** for 5 minutes or until heated through. Let stand, covered, for 5 minutes before serving.

Stir remaining glaze into pan drippings; pour into a serving bowl. Pass at the table to spoon over individual slices. Makes 4 to 6 servings.

SPICY SAUSAGE SAUTÉ

Chilled applesauce offers a refreshing counterpoint to this colorful, spicy medley of vegetables and sausage slices.

Choose one or a combination of fully cooked sausages, such as kielbasa (Polish sausage), knackwurst (garlic frankfurters), smoked sausage links, bratwurst, frankfurters, or cooked pork sausage links.

3 tablespoons butter or margarine
4 teaspoons curry powder
1 large white onion, cut in wedges and layers separated
1 large green pepper, seeded and cut into 1-inch squares
1 to 1¼ pounds fully cooked sausages, cut into ½-inch slanting slices
2 medium-size tomatoes, cut into wedges
1 can (1 lb.) applesauce, chilled
Ground cinnamon or nutmeg

Microwave a 10-inch browning dish on **HIGH (100%)** for 4 minutes. Carefully remove dish (the bottom is very hot) to a heat-proof surface. Add butter and curry powder; stir until butter is melted and bubbly. Add onion and green pepper, stirring to coat with curry butter. Microwave, uncovered, on **HIGH (100%)** for 3 minutes.

Stir in sausage slices. Cover with a glass lid. Microwave on **HIGH (100%)** for 4 minutes (stirring after 2 minutes) or until sausages are heated through. Stir in tomato wedges. Microwave, covered, on **HIGH (100%)** for 2 minutes. Let stand, covered, for 5 minutes. Stir well before serving.

Spoon applesauce into a serving bowl, sprinkle lightly with cinnamon, and pass at the table. Makes 4 servings.

SIMMERED COUNTRY-STYLE RIBS

To take full advantage of the generous amount of sauce, accompany the meat with noodles or potatoes.

¾ cup dry red wine
¼ cup water
½ cup tomato-based chili sauce or catsup
3 tablespoons *each* brown sugar and cider vinegar
1 tablespoon Worcestershire
½ teaspoon *each* dry mustard and chili powder
2½ to 3 pounds country-style spareribs
1 teaspoon paprika
1 medium-size onion, sliced
1 small red or green bell pepper, seeded and cut into strips
2½ tablespoons *each* cornstarch and water
1 package (10 oz.) frozen peas

In a 2-cup glass measure, combine wine, water, chili sauce, sugar, vinegar, Worcestershire, mustard, and chili powder; blend well. Microwave, uncovered, on **HIGH (100%)** for 4 minutes.

Meanwhile, sprinkle spareribs with paprika and rub into meat. Place in a 7 by 11-inch baking dish. Distribute onion around meat and pour warm wine mixture over all. Cover with plastic wrap. Microwave on **HIGH (100%)** for 10 minutes. Turn ribs over. Microwave, covered, on **MEDIUM (50%)** for 20 minutes.

Turn ribs over again and add pepper strips. Microwave, covered, on **MEDIUM (50%)** for 25 to 30 minutes or until meat in thickest portion is no longer pink when slashed. Let stand, covered, for 5 minutes. Transfer meat to a platter; cover.

Stir together cornstarch and water. Skim excess fat from drippings and add cornstarch mixture. Microwave, uncovered, on **HIGH (100%)** for 3 minutes, stirring after 2 minutes. Add peas. Microwave, uncovered, on **HIGH (100%)** for 3 to 4 minutes (stirring after 2 minutes) or until sauce is thickened and peas are tender.

Spoon some of the sauce over ribs; pass remaining sauce at the table. Makes 4 servings.

HEARTY HOT SANDWICHES

Take your pick — on this page we present a sandwich for every taste, from savory sausage laced with apple and sauerkraut to sautéed mushrooms topped with tomatoes and cheese, or a toasty grilled cheese sandwich.

SAUSAGE & SAUERKRAUT POCKETS

(Pictured on page 31)

The ingredients are international, and the merger is extraordinary. These hearty pocket sandwiches, chock-full of Polish sausage, sweet apple, French mustard, and sauerkraut, make a satisfying meal. Pocket bread (also called peda or pita) is available in most supermarkets or in Middle Eastern food stores.

   1 tablespoon butter or margarine
   3 kielbasa sausages, cut into ½-inch slices
   1 medium-size onion, sliced
   1 large red-skinned apple, cored and diced
   1 can (8 oz.) sauerkraut, drained well
  ¼ cup sweet pickle relish
   1 tablespoon Dijon mustard
   3 pocket breads, halved

Microwave a 10-inch browning dish on **HIGH (100%)** for 4½ minutes. Carefully remove dish (the bottom is very hot) to a heatproof surface. Add butter and swirl until bottom is coated. Add sausages and stir until browned on all sides; then stir in onion. Cover with a glass lid. Microwave on **HIGH (100%)** for 3 minutes. Stir in apple, sauerkraut, pickle relish, and mustard. Microwave, covered, on **HIGH (100%)** for 2 minutes. Let stand, covered, while heating bread.

Wrap bread halves in paper towels. Microwave on **HIGH (100%)** for 15 to 30 seconds or until heated through. Spoon sausage mixture evenly into bread pockets and serve immediately. Makes 6 sandwiches.

MUSHROOM & CHEESE SANDWICHES

Layer sautéed mushrooms, tomatoes, and cheese for these simple but special open-faced sandwiches. Serve them hot with a cup of onion soup or with fresh fruit of the season.

   2 tablespoons butter or margarine
  ½ pound mushrooms, sliced
  ⅛ teaspoon *each* salt and pepper
   4 slices light rye bread, toasted and buttered
   2 medium-size tomatoes, seeded and sliced
   6 ounces sliced jack cheese
    Chopped parsley

Place butter in a 9-inch nonmetallic pie plate. Microwave, uncovered, on **HIGH (100%)** for 30 seconds or until butter is melted. Stir in mushrooms. Microwave, uncovered, on **HIGH (100%)** for 7 to 8 minutes (stirring every 3 minutes) or until liquid evaporates. Sprinkle with salt and pepper. Reserving 8 mushroom slices for garnish, evenly distribute remaining mushrooms over bread slices. Arrange tomato slices over mushrooms, and cover evenly with cheese.

Place 2 reserved mushrooms on top of each sandwich; sprinkle with parsley. Place sandwiches on a flat 10 or 12-inch plate. Microwave, uncovered, on **HIGH (100%)** for 2 minutes or until cheese is melted. Makes 4 open-faced sandwiches.

GRILLED CHEESE SANDWICH

With a browning skillet as your grill, you can create a golden brown melted cheese sandwich in just 6 minutes.

   2 slices process American cheese
   2 slices bread
    Butter or margarine

Place cheese between bread slices; butter outside of each bread slice. Microwave a browning skillet or dish on **HIGH (100%)** for 4 minutes. Carefully remove skillet (the bottom is very hot) to a heatproof surface. Place sandwich in hot skillet and press down with a spatula for 30 seconds; turn sandwich over and brown for 30 more seconds. Microwave, uncovered, on **HIGH (100%)** for 45 seconds or until cheese is melted. Let stand for 1 minute. Makes 1 sandwich.

PORK CHOPS & DUMPLINGS

Combine apple juice with cream of mushroom soup and you have a rich and creamy sauce for this easy entrée. Homemade herb dumplings, so adaptable to microwave cooking, crown each pork chop. Serve them with a green salad tossed with vinaigrette dressing.

    4 loin pork chops, *each*
       1 inch thick
    1 teaspoon *each* ground sage
       and paprika
    ⅓ cup apple juice
    1 can (10¾ oz.) condensed cream
       of mushroom soup
    1 cup all-purpose flour
    1¼ teaspoons baking powder
    1 tablespoon *each* instant
       minced onion and
       chopped parsley
    ¼ teaspoon salt
    2 tablespoons firm butter
       or margarine
    ½ cup milk

Trim excess fat from chops. Rub sage and paprika evenly over both sides of chops. Arrange in a 9-inch square baking dish with meaty portions to outside of dish. In a small bowl, combine apple juice and soup; pour over meat. Cover with plastic wrap.

Microwave on **HIGH (100%)** for 12 to 13 minutes (turning chops over and basting with soup mixture after 6 minutes) or until meat near bone is no longer pink when slashed.

Meanwhile, in a small bowl, stir together flour, baking powder, onion, parsley, and salt. With a pastry blender or two knives, cut butter into flour mixture until it resembles coarse crumbs. Add milk and stir just to moisten dry ingredients.

Spoon batter equally over cooked chops. Cover with wax paper. Microwave on **HIGH (100%)** for 6 to 7 minutes (rotating dish ¼ turn after 4 minutes) or until a wooden pick inserted in center of dumpling comes out clean. Makes 4 servings.

PERSIAN LAMB WITH PEACHES

(Pictured on facing page)

Juicy peach slices accent spicy morsels of lamb with a refreshing hint of sweetness. Tangy yogurt adds a note of delicious contrast to this Middle Eastern dish. Serve lamb over rice and garnish with mint, if desired.

       About 1 pound peaches or
         nectarines, or 1 can (1 lb.) sliced
         peaches, drained well
       Lemon juice
       About 2 pounds lean boneless
         lamb shoulder
    1 teaspoon ground cinnamon
    ½ teaspoon ground cloves
    ¼ teaspoon pepper
    2 tablespoons brown sugar
    1 medium-size onion, chopped
    2 tablespoons lemon juice
    4 teaspoons *each* cornstarch and
         water
       Salt
       Hot cooked rice
       Mint leaves (optional)
       Unflavored yogurt

Peel and pit peaches; cut into thick slices. Sprinkle with lemon juice. (If using canned peaches, omit lemon juice.) Set peaches aside.

Trim excess fat from lamb; cut meat into ¾-inch cubes. Arrange in a shallow 2-quart baking dish. Mix together cinnamon, cloves, pepper, and sugar; sprinkle over lamb. Add onion and the 2 tablespoons lemon juice. Cover with a lid or plastic wrap.

Microwave on **HIGH (100%)** for 5 minutes; stir well. Microwave, covered, on **MEDIUM (50%)** for 30 minutes (stirring after 15 minutes) or until meat is fork-tender. Let stand, covered, for 5 minutes. Transfer lamb to a plate and cover. Stir together cornstarch and water; then stir into lamb juices. Microwave, uncovered, on **HIGH (100%)** for 2 to 3 minutes (stirring every minute) or until bubbly and thickened. Season to taste with salt and stir in meat, then spoon over hot cooked rice. Garnish with peaches and mint. Pass yogurt to spoon over individual servings. Makes 4 to 6 servings.

HERBED LAMB SHANKS

A tasty, herb-laced wine and tomato sauce flavors these tender lamb shanks. Cooked on half power **(50%)**, the meaty shanks become tender in half the time it would take to cook them conventionally.

    4 lamb shanks (about 1 lb. *each*),
         with bones cracked
    1 large onion, sliced
    1 large green pepper, seeded
         and thinly sliced
    1 can (6 oz.) tomato juice
    ½ cup dry red wine
    2 cloves garlic, minced
         or pressed
    1 teaspoon *each* thyme and
         savory leaves
    ¼ teaspoon pepper
    2 tablespoons *each* cornstarch
         and water
       Salt

(Continued on next page)

Place lamb shanks in a 7 by 11-inch baking dish with meaty portions to outside of dish. Distribute onion and green pepper slices over and around shanks.

In a small bowl, stir together tomato juice, wine, garlic, thyme, savory, and pepper; pour over shanks. Cover with pleated plastic wrap (page 7). Microwave on **MEDIUM (50%)** for 1¼ hours or until shanks are fork-tender.

With a slotted spoon, transfer shanks to a rimmed serving platter and top with vegetables. Skim off and discard fat from juices in dish. Stir together cornstarch and water. With a wire whip, blend into juices along with salt to taste. Microwave, uncovered, on **HIGH (100%)** for 4 minutes (stirring after 2 minutes) or until sauce thickens. Pour over shanks. Makes 4 servings.

CHICKEN IN TARRAGON CREAM

Cloaked in a piquant sour cream sauce laced with green onions and tarragon, chicken breasts bake to a succulent goodness. Serve with a mound of fluffy rice, and brighten each serving with broccoli spears and cherry tomatoes.

- ½ cup *each* dry white wine and sour cream
- 1 clove garlic, minced or pressed
- ¼ teaspoon dry tarragon
- 1 tablespoon *each* lemon juice and thinly sliced green onion (including top)
- 2 teaspoons sugar
- ½ teaspoon salt
- 1 teaspoon cornstarch
  Dash of white pepper
- 1 tablespoon butter, margarine, or salad oil
- 2 large whole chicken breasts (about 2¼ lbs. *total*), split, skinned, and boned
  Chopped parsley

Measure wine in a 2-cup glass measure. Stir in sour cream, garlic, tarragon, lemon juice, onion, sugar, salt, cornstarch, and pepper. Microwave, uncovered, on **HIGH (100%)** for 2 minutes (stirring after 1 minute) or until slightly thickened; set aside.

Microwave a 10-inch browning dish on **HIGH (100%)** for 4½ minutes. Carefully remove dish (the bottom is very hot) to a heatproof surface. Add butter and tilt dish to coat bottom evenly. Add chicken breasts. Let brown for about 30 seconds on each side.

Microwave, uncovered, on **HIGH (100%)** for 2 minutes. Rotate each chicken breast ½ turn; pour sauce over chicken. Microwave on **MEDIUM (50%)** for 2 to 3 minutes or until juices run clear when meat is slashed. Spoon sauce over each breast and sprinkle with parsley; let stand for 5 minutes before serving. Makes 2 to 4 servings.

KAUAI CHICKEN

Hoisin sauce, the traditional mahogany-hued accompaniment to Peking duck, imparts a distinctively sweet and spicy flavor to chicken as well. Look for the sauce in Oriental markets or in the specialty section of your supermarket.

You'll need only a small amount of the hoisin sauce, but the unused portion can be stored, covered, in the refrigerator almost indefinitely.

- ⅓ cup soy sauce
- 3 tablespoons *each* granulated sugar and brown sugar
- 2 tablespoons hoisin sauce
- ⅛ teaspoon garlic salt
- 1 broiler-fryer chicken (3 lbs.), skinned and cut into pieces

In a small bowl, combine soy, granulated and brown sugars,

hoisin, and garlic salt; blend well. Arrange chicken pieces in a 7 by 11-inch baking dish with meaty portions to outside of dish. Pour soy mixture evenly over chicken.

Let chicken marinate for 15 minutes. Pour off and reserve marinade. Cover chicken with wax paper. Microwave on **HIGH (100%)** for 8 minutes. Turn chicken over and brush with reserved marinade. Microwave, covered, on **HIGH (100%)** for 8 to 9 minutes or until meat near thigh bone is no longer pink when slashed. Let stand, covered, for 5 minutes before serving. Makes 4 servings.

SWISS CHICKEN

For a special occasion or for everyday fare, chicken breasts serve two in an elegant fashion. Round out the menu with a tossed green salad and with buttered noodles you can start cooking as you bone the chicken breasts. In just 30 minutes the entire meal will be ready.

- 1 large whole chicken breast (about 1 lb.), split, skinned, and boned
- ¼ teaspoon *each* salt and paprika
- 1 teaspoon cornstarch
- 2 tablespoons cream sherry
- ⅓ cup whipping cream
- ½ cup shredded Swiss cheese
  Chopped parsley

Place chicken, skinned side up, in a 1-quart baking dish. In a small bowl, combine salt, paprika, and cornstarch; stir in sherry and cream; blend well. Pour sauce over chicken. Cover dish with a lid or plastic wrap. Microwave on **MEDIUM-HIGH (70%)** for 4 minutes, stirring sauce after 2 minutes and spooning it over chicken.

Rotate each chicken breast ½ turn; spoon sauce over chicken.

(Continued on next page)

Microwave, covered, on **MEDIUM-HIGH (70%)** for 1 minute or until juices run clear when meat is slashed.

Sprinkle chicken with cheese and parsley. Microwave, uncovered, on **HIGH (100%)** for 30 seconds or until cheese melts. Let stand for 5 minutes before serving. Makes 2 servings.

CHICKEN DIVAN RAMEKINS

(Pictured on page 39)

It's hard to believe that such elegance is so easy to accomplish.

- 1 can (10¾ oz.) condensed cream of chicken soup
- 3 tablespoons *each* mayonnaise and milk
- ¼ teaspoon prepared mustard
- 2 packages (about 10 oz. *each*) frozen chopped broccoli
- 3 to 4 cups shredded cooked chicken or turkey
- 1 cup (4 oz.) shredded Cheddar cheese

In a small bowl, combine soup, mayonnaise, milk, and mustard; blend well, then set aside.

Microwave broccoli according to package directions. Drain off excess water, then divide broccoli among four 10-ounce ramekins, spreading broccoli on bottom and up sides of each ramekin. Arrange chicken pieces over broccoli, then evenly spoon soup mixture over chicken. Cover each ramekin with plastic wrap. (At this point you may refrigerate until next day.)

Place ramekins in a square and microwave, covered, on **HIGH (100%)** for 10 minutes (turning each dish ¼ turn after 5 minutes) or until sauce is bubbly. (If refrigerated, microwave on **HIGH (100%)** for 12 to 15 minutes.) Uncover and sprinkle with cheese. Let stand for 5 minutes. Makes 4 servings.

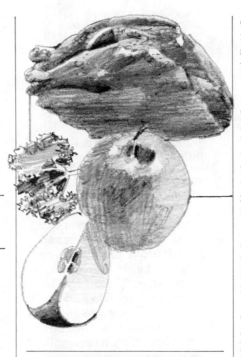

CHICKEN CURRY

This speedy entrée turns leftover meat into exotic company fare. Use chicken, turkey, lamb, beef — even canned shrimp. Spoon the savory mixture over hot cooked rice.

- 2 tablespoons butter or margarine
- 1 medium-size onion, chopped
- 2 teaspoons *each* curry powder and sugar
- ½ teaspoon ground ginger
- 2 chicken or beef bouillon cubes dissolved in ½ cup hot water
- 1 small red-skinned apple, chopped
- 1 can (10¾ oz.) condensed cream of chicken or mushroom soup
- 1 teaspoon lemon juice
- 2 to 3 cups cooked chicken, turkey, lamb, or beef, cut into bite-size pieces, or 2 cans (4½ oz. *each*) deveined medium-size shrimp, rinsed and drained
  Hot cooked rice
  Condiments (suggestions follow)

Place butter in a 2-quart casserole. Microwave, uncovered, on **HIGH (100%)** for 1 minute. Stir in onion. Microwave, un-

covered, on **HIGH (100%)** for 3 mintues. Stir in curry powder, sugar, and ginger. Microwave, uncovered, on **HIGH (100%)** for 1 minute.

Add bouillon to onion mixture along with apple, soup, and lemon juice; blend well. Cover with a lid or wax paper. Microwave on **HIGH (100%)** for 3 minutes. Stir in chicken. Microwave, covered, on **HIGH (100%)** for 2 to 3 minutes or until heated through.

Spoon individual servings over rice. At the table, pass your choice of condiments in individual bowls. Makes 4 servings.

Condiments.   Cooked and crumbled bacon, chopped hard-cooked egg, sliced banana, salted peanuts, shredded coconut, diced tomato, diced avocado, raisins, and chutney.

CHICKEN WITH PLUM SAUCE

With just one can of purple plums, you make enough tangy sauce for two meals. Spoon it over chicken; another time, brush it over pork roast (page 30).

- 1 can (1 lb.) whole purple plums
- 2 tablespoons butter or margarine
- 1 medium-size onion, finely chopped
- ¼ cup firmly packed brown sugar
- ¼ cup tomato-based chili sauce
- 2 tablespoons soy sauce
- 1 teaspoon ground ginger
- 2 teaspoons lemon juice
- 1 whole broiler-fryer chicken (3 to 3½ lbs.)
  Salt and pepper

Drain plums, reserving 2 tablespoons of the syrup; remove pits. Place plums and reserved syrup in a blender and whirl until puréed; set aside.

Place butter in a 1-quart casserole. Microwave, uncovered, on **HIGH (100%)** for 1 minute; stir in onion and microwave on **HIGH (100%)** for 2 more minutes. Stir in sugar, chili sauce, soy, ginger, lemon juice, and plum purée. Microwave, uncovered, on **HIGH (100%)** for 5 minutes (stirring every 2 minutes) or until sauce thickens slightly; set aside.

Remove giblets from chicken; set aside for other uses. Rinse chicken and pat dry. Sprinkle cavity with salt and pepper. Place chicken, breast side down, on a nonmetallic rack in a 7 by 11-inch baking dish.

Microwave, uncovered, on **HIGH (100%)** for 12 minutes, brushing generously with sauce after 6 minutes. Turn breast side up. Microwave, uncovered, on **HIGH (100%)** for 12 minutes (brushing generously with sauce after 6 minutes) or until juices run clear and meat near thigh bone is no longer pink when slashed.

Transfer chicken to a serving platter; cover very loosely with foil and let stand for 5 minutes before serving.

Pour juices from baking dish into a small bowl; skim off and discard fat. Stir in about ⅓ cup of the plum sauce (cover and refrigerate remaining sauce, reserving for other uses). Microwave, uncovered, on **HIGH (100%)** for 1 minute or until heated through.

Pass sauce at the table to spoon over individual servings. Makes 4 servings.

GAME HENS WITH APRICOTS

(Pictured on front cover)

Apricot preserves impart a mildly sweet fruity accent to these miniature birds; fresh apricots add contrast.

2 Rock Cornish game hens (20 to 24 oz. *each*), thawed
2 tablespoons bottled brown gravy sauce mixed with 2 tablespoons water
½ cup apricot preserves
¼ teaspoon prepared mustard
1 tablespoon dry sherry
1 teaspoon lemon juice
1 pound apricots, cut in half, pitted, and sprinkled with lemon juice, or 1 can (1 lb.) apricot halves, drained well
Watercress (optional)

Remove giblets from hens and set aside for other uses. Brush hens with gravy mixture. Place birds, breast side down, on a nonmetallic rack in a 7 by 11-inch baking dish. Cover with wax paper. Microwave on **HIGH (100%)** for 6 minutes. Turn hens over and brush with remaining gravy mixture. Microwave, covered, on **HIGH (100%)** for 6 more minutes.

Meanwhile, in a small bowl, stir together apricot preserves, mustard, sherry, and lemon juice. Brush hens with some of the apricot glaze. Microwave, uncovered, on **HIGH (100%)** for 3 minutes. Turn birds over and brush with more apricot glaze. Microwave, uncovered, on **HIGH (100%)** for 3 more minutes or until meat near thigh bone is no longer pink when slashed. Cover very loosely with foil and let stand for 5 minutes.

Just before serving, gently stir apricot halves into remaining apricot glaze. Microwave, uncovered, on **HIGH (100%)** for 1 to 2 minutes or until heated through. Arrange glazed apricots around hens. Garnish with watercress, if desired. Makes 2 to 4 servings.

TURKEY WITH CASHEW BUTTER

For an elegant buffet, consider this boneless turkey breast,

carved into thick slices and drizzled with cashew-studded butter.

½ turkey breast (about 3½ lbs.), boned and skinned, (thawed if frozen)
   Ground nutmeg and pepper
½ cup butter or margarine
¼ teaspoon grated lemon peel
2½ teaspoons lemon juice
½ cup coarsely chopped, salted cashews
   Parsley sprigs
   Lemon wedges

Generously sprinkle turkey with nutmeg and pepper. Place in a 7 by 11-inch baking dish; cover with plastic wrap. Microwave on **HIGH (100%)** for 14 minutes, turning meat over after 7 minutes. Let stand, covered, for 7 minutes. Juices should run clear and meat in thickest portion should no longer be pink when slashed.

If meat is not done to your liking, microwave, covered, on **HIGH (100%)** for 2 to 4 more minutes, checking for doneness after 2 minutes.

Place butter in a 2-cup glass measure. Microwave, uncovered, on **HIGH (100%)** for 1 minute or until melted and bubbly. Stir in lemon peel, lemon juice, and cashews.

To serve, cut meat into ¼ to ⅜-inch-thick slices. Arrange on a rimmed serving platter. Stir through nut butter, then pour over meat. Microwave, uncovered, on **HIGH (100%)** for 1½ to 2 minutes or until heated through. Garnish with parsley and lemon wedges. Keep hot on an electric warming tray, if desired. Makes 6 to 8 servings.

Handsome Chicken Divan Ramekins (page 37) only look elaborate. With the microwave, they're a cinch to prepare. They can even be assembled ahead of time and heated briefly just before serving. Accompany them with a lettuce and fruit salad and bakery rolls.

DRESSING UP THE BIRD

For chicken that's as handsome in appearance as it is succulent in taste, dress up the bird by wrapping it in one of our well-seasoned, colorful crumb mixtures. The chicken pieces bake to showy perfection in just minutes — crisp and appealing on the outside, tender and moist on the inside.

OVEN-FRIED CHICKEN

Simply roll chicken pieces in melted butter and then dredge them in one of our crumb-based coatings. We recommend microwaving the chicken on a nonmetallic rack to prevent the bottom from getting soggy as the top crisps — and there's no need to turn the pieces over.

    2 chicken legs, with thighs attached, and 1 whole chicken breast, split (about 2 lbs. *total*)
    2 tablespoons butter or margarine
      Crumb coating (recipes follow)

Rinse chicken pieces; pat dry with paper towels and set aside.

Place butter in a 7 by 11-inch baking dish. Microwave, uncovered, on **HIGH (100%)** for 30 seconds or until butter is bubbly. Roll chicken pieces in butter and drain briefly; shake in crumb coating or press coating evenly onto chicken. Arrange pieces, skin side up, on a nonmetallic rack placed in baking dish, with meaty portions of thighs to outside of rack and breasts in center.

Microwave, uncovered, on **HIGH (100%)** for 7 to 9 minutes (rotating dish ¼ turn after 3½ minutes) or until juices run clear and meat near thigh bone is no longer pink when slashed. Let stand for 5 minutes before serving. Makes 4 or 5 servings.

Parmesan-coated chicken. In a bag, combine 2 tablespoons *each* grated **Parmesan cheese** and **yellow cornmeal**, 3 tablespoons fine dry **bread crumbs**, ½ teaspoon *each* **garlic salt** and **oregano leaves**, and ¼ teaspoon **paprika**.

Paprika-coated chicken. In a bag, combine 6 tablespoons **all-purpose flour**, 2 teaspoons *each* **paprika** and **poultry seasoning**, and ½ teaspoon *each* **salt** and **garlic powder**.

Stuffing-coated chicken. In a bag, combine ⅔ cup finely crushed **packaged stuffing mix** or herb seasoned croutons and 1 tablespoon **parsley flakes**.

Onion and sage-coated chicken. In a 9-inch pie plate, combine 1 can (3 oz.) **French-fried onions** (crumbled), 2 tablespoons fine dry **bread crumbs**, 1 tablespoon **parsley flakes**, and ½ teaspoon **ground sage**. Press coating onto chicken.

CORNFLAKE-COATED CHICKEN

Cornflake crumbs with a hint of rosemary and garlic coat these oven-fried chicken pieces.

    1 cup cornflake crumbs
    ½ teaspoon *each* crushed dry rosemary and garlic salt
    ¼ teaspoon paprika
    1 broiler-fryer chicken (about 3 lbs.), cut into pieces and skinned
    2 eggs, lightly beaten
    4 tablespoons butter or margarine

In a 9-inch pie plate, combine cornflake crumbs, rosemary, garlic salt, and paprika. Coat chicken with beaten eggs; roll in crumb mixture. Arrange chicken in a 7 by 11-inch baking dish with meaty portions to outside of dish.

Place butter in a 10-ounce custard cup and microwave, uncovered, on **HIGH (100%)** for 1 minute. Drizzle 2 tablespoons of the butter over chicken. Cover with wax paper. Microwave on **HIGH (100%)** for 8 minutes. Turn pieces over and drizzle with remaining 2 tablespoons butter. Microwave, covered on **HIGH (100%)** for 8 to 10 minutes or until meat near thigh bone is no longer pink when slashed. Let stand, covered, for 5 minutes. Makes 4 servings.

TURKEY LEGS TERIYAKI

Turkey drumsticks marinate overnight in a lemon-soy mixture that later becomes a flavorful sauce to spoon over the cooked meat. Steamed brown rice and green beans are fitting accompaniments.

¼ cup *each* soy sauce and water
2 tablespoons *each* dry sherry and lemon juice
1 tablespoon sugar
2 teaspoons finely minced fresh ginger
2 cloves garlic, minced or pressed
½ teaspoon grated lemon peel
Dash of pepper
2 large turkey drumsticks (about 1¼ lbs. *each*)
2 tablespoons cornstarch
⅓ cup chicken broth

In a 1-cup glass measure, combine soy, water, sherry, lemon juice, sugar, ginger, garlic, lemon peel, and pepper; blend well. Place turkey legs in a 7 by 11-inch baking dish. Pour soy mixture over meat and cover. Refrigerate overnight, turning meat over at least twice.

To cook, drain marinade into a 2-cup glass measure; set aside. Cover baking dish with plastic wrap. Microwave on **HIGH (100%)** for 10 minutes. Turn legs over. Microwave, covered, on **MEDIUM-LOW (30%)** for 40 minutes, turning meat over after 20 minutes. Let stand, covered, for 15 minutes. Meat near bone should no longer be pink when slashed.

If meat is not done to your liking, microwave, covered, on **MEDIUM-LOW (30%)** for 4 to 8 more minutes, checking for doneness after 4 minutes.

Microwave reserved marinade, uncovered, on **HIGH (100%)** for 2 minutes or until boiling. Stir together cornstarch and broth; add to marinade and microwave, uncovered, on **HIGH (100%)** for 2 minutes (stirring after 1 minute) or until mixture thickens. Pass at the table to spoon over individual servings. Makes 2 servings.

TURKEY-TORTILLA CASSEROLE

Sure to become an after-the-holidays favorite, this colorful and spirited entrée combines diced turkey, ripe olives, two kinds of cheese, and corn tortilla strips.

4 cups diced cooked turkey or chicken
1 can (10¾ oz.) condensed cream of mushroom soup
1 can (4 oz.) diced green chili peppers, drained
1 can (7 oz.) green chili salsa
1 can (2¼ oz.) sliced ripe olives, drained
⅓ cup thinly sliced green onions (including tops)
¾ teaspoon ground cumin
8 corn tortillas, cut into ½-inch strips
2 cups (8 oz.) *each* shredded jack and Cheddar cheeses

In a bowl, combine turkey, soup, chili peppers, salsa, olives, onions, and cumin.

Arrange half the tortilla strips in a well-greased 7 by 11-inch baking dish. Cover evenly with half the turkey mixture; sprinkle with jack cheese. Top with remaining tortilla strips and turkey mixture. Cover with plastic wrap. Microwave on **HIGH (100%)** for 10 minutes (rotating dish ½ turn after 5 minutes) or until heated through.

Sprinkle with Cheddar cheese. Microwave, covered, on **HIGH (100%)** for 1 minute. Let stand, covered, for 5 minutes before serving. Makes 6 to 8 servings.

SCALLOPS IN CHEDDAR SAUCE

Bathed in a wine and cheese sauce, tender scallops and fresh sliced mushrooms make an impressive entrée for a special brunch or dinner party.

3 tablespoons butter or margarine
½ pound mushrooms, sliced
1 pound scallops, rinsed and cut into bite-size pieces
About ½ cup dry white wine
2 tablespoons all-purpose flour
¼ teaspoon salt
½ cup shredded sharp Cheddar cheese
Chopped parsley

Place 1 tablespoon of the butter in a 9 or 10-inch glass pie plate. Microwave, uncovered, on **HIGH (100%)** for 30 seconds. Stir in mushrooms. Microwave, uncovered, on **HIGH (100%)** for 4 minutes (stirring after 2 minutes) or until soft. With a slotted spoon, lift out mushrooms and set aside. Drain off liquid.

In same dish, place scallops and ½ cup of the wine. Cover with plastic wrap. Microwave on **HIGH (100%)** for 2½ to 3 minutes (stirring every minute) or until scallops are opaque throughout. With a slotted spoon, lift out scallops and set aside. Drain poaching liquid into a 1-cup glass measure; you should have 1 cup. If not, add wine to make 1 cup total.

Place remaining 2 tablespoons butter in dish. Microwave, uncovered, on **HIGH (100%)** for 30 seconds. Stir in flour and salt. Microwave, uncovered, on **HIGH (100%)** for 1 minute or until bubbly. Slowly stir in poaching liquid. Microwave, uncovered, on **HIGH (100%)** for 3 minutes (stirring every minute) or until sauce is bubbly and thickened. Add cheese and stir until melted;

(Continued on page 43)

stir in mushrooms and scallops. Spoon mixture into 4 scallop shells or individual ramekins. (At this point you may cover and refrigerate until next day.)

To serve, microwave, uncovered, on **HIGH (100%)** for 1 to 1½ minutes (2 to 2½ minutes, if refrigerated) or until heated through. Garnish each serving with parsley. Makes 4 servings.

CRAB IN SPICY TOMATO SAUCE

(Pictured on facing page)

For this delicious — but messy — finger food, combine a zesty sauce and pieces of crab in the shell.

When the last shell is emptied, provide lemon-scented hot towels from the microwave. Here's how: wet towels and wring out excess moisture; sprinkle lightly with lemon juice, roll up, and microwave on **HIGH (100%)** for 1 to 2 minutes.

- 1 cup catsup
- ½ cup hot water
- 2 whole cloves
- ½ teaspoon seasoned salt
- ¼ teaspoon *each* thyme leaves and sugar
- 1½ teaspoons Worcestershire
- ½ teaspoon prepared horseradish
- 1 bay leaf
- 1 large Dungeness crab (about 2 lbs.), cleaned and cracked

In a 1½ or 2-quart baking dish, combine catsup, water, cloves, seasoned salt, thyme, sugar, Worcestershire, horseradish, and bay leaf. Microwave, uncovered, on **HIGH (100%)** for 2 minutes (stirring after 1 minute) or until bubbly. Add crab

Saucy with spices, this cracked crab supper includes crusty French bread for soaking up the rich flavors. Add your favorite crunchy cole slaw to this Crab in Spicy Tomato Sauce entrée (recipe above) for a cool flavor contrast.

pieces. Microwave, uncovered, on **HIGH (100%)** for 2 minutes or until heated through.

Serve crab and sauce in individual bowls. Makes 2 servings.

CARROT-TOPPED POACHED FISH

There's no need to defrost these frozen fish fillets. Simply take the fish out of the freezer, thaw slightly in the microwave, and poach them together with a shredded carrot topping.

- 3 tablespoons butter or margarine
- 1 cup coarsely shredded carrots
- ½ teaspoon grated lemon peel
- 1 tablespoon lemon juice
- ¼ teaspoon thyme leaves
- 1 package (1 lb.) frozen fish fillets (sole, cod, perch, or haddock)
- 1 tablespoon all-purpose flour
- 3 tablespoons whipping cream

Place 2 tablespoons of the butter in a 9-inch square baking dish. Microwave, uncovered, on **HIGH (100%)** for 30 seconds. Stir in carrots, lemon peel, lemon juice, and thyme. Push vegetable mixture to one side.

Lay two paper towels on floor of microwave. Place fish package on towels and microwave on **MEDIUM (50%)** for 4 minutes, turning package over after 2 minutes. Unwrap fish and cut block in half. Place in bottom of baking dish and spoon carrot mixture over each piece. Cover with plastic wrap.

Microwave on **HIGH (100%)** for 4 minutes. Rotate each fish piece ½ turn. Let stand, covered, for 5 minutes. Microwave, covered, on **HIGH (100%)** for 4 more minutes or until fish flakes readily when prodded with a fork. Transfer fish to a serving platter and cover.

To cooking liquid, add the

remaining 1 tablespoon butter and flour. Beat with a wire whip until smooth. Microwave, uncovered, on **HIGH (100%)** for 2 minutes or until sauce is bubbly and thickened. Stir in cream and pour over fish. Makes 2 servings.

FISH IN VEGETABLE SAUCE

First make the tangy sauce, then add the fish pieces, and bake them together to delicious perfection.

- 2 tablespoons butter or margarine
- 1 small onion, cut into thin rings
- ¼ pound mushrooms, sliced
- 1 medium-size tomato, seeded and chopped
- ¼ teaspoon oregano leaves
- ⅓ cup tomato-based chili sauce
- 1 pound red snapper or lingcod fillets (about ½ inch thick)
- ⅓ cup grated Parmesan cheese

Place butter in a 7 by 11-inch baking dish. Microwave, uncovered, on **HIGH (100%)** for 30 seconds. Separate onion rings and stir into butter. Microwave, uncovered, on **HIGH (100%)** for 3 minutes. Add mushrooms, tomato, oregano, and chili sauce; stir well. Microwave, uncovered, on **HIGH (100%)** for 7 minutes, stirring after 4 minutes.

Cut fish into serving-size pieces. Push vegetable sauce to one side. Arrange fish in a single layer on bottom of dish with meaty portions to outside of dish. Spoon sauce over fish.

Microwave, uncovered, on **HIGH (100%)** for 3 minutes, rotating each fish piece ½ turn after 2 minutes. Sprinkle with cheese. Let stand for 3 minutes. Fish should flake easily with a fork. If not done to your liking, microwave on **HIGH (100%)** for 1 more minute. Makes 4 servings.

Our recipes will take your children through the day, from a breakfast of oatmeal and baked apples to an after-dinner treat of S'mores. And all the instructions are written so the kids can do it themselves. Where kids are concerned, the microwave is a special boon, the key to culinary independence when the occasion calls for it. Once they're instructed in the use of the microwave and the proper utensils, children can easily manage their own light meals and snacks.

CINNAMON BAKED APPLE

Red cinnamon candies turn an apple into a tasty treat. Serve it for breakfast, a nutritious snack, or dessert.

    1 small tart apple
    1 tablespoon tiny red cinnamon candies

Core apple and place in a 6-ounce custard cup. Fill hollow center with candies. Cover with wax paper. Microwave on **HIGH (100%)** for 2½ to 3 minutes, rotating dish ¼ turn after 2 minutes. Let stand, uncovered, for 5 minutes. Apple should be fork-tender when pierced. If not, cover and microwave on **HIGH (100%)** for 1 to 2 more minutes. Spoon melted candy sauce over apple. Makes 1 serving.

QUICK HOT OATMEAL

No matter what the weather outside, a bowl of steaming oatmeal is always welcome at breakfast. Cereal can boil over, so be sure to make it in a 2-cup or larger dish. Orange wedges or banana chunks and a tall glass of milk complete the meal.

    ½ cup quick-cooking rolled oats
    1 cup water
    ¼ teaspoon salt
       Butter, ground cinnamon, brown sugar or maple syrup, and milk (optional)

In a 2-cup nonmetallic cereal bowl, stir together oats, water, and salt. Microwave, uncovered, on

HIGH (100%) for 1½ to 2 minutes or until liquid is absorbed. Stir, then let stand, uncovered, for 2 minutes before eating. Add butter, cinnamon, brown sugar, and milk, if desired. Makes 1 serving.

HOT DOGS IN BUNS

In just 45 seconds, the microwave turns out a frankfurter cooked in a bun, ready to adorn with mustard, catsup, pickle relish, or other favorite trimmings. If both meat and bun are frozen, simply double the cooking time.

For each serving, place a frankfurter in a bun. Wrap bun in a paper towel or napkin and place on floor of microwave. Microwave on **HIGH (100%)** for 45 seconds or until heated through.

To microwave more than 1 at a time, determine total cooking time. Arrange 2 side by side, 3 in a triangle, 4 in a square, 5 or 6 spoke-fashion.

BUBBLY CHEESE & CRACKERS

Cubes of cheese melt on crackers for a quick and easy snack. For a speedy lunch, serve them alongside a mug of hot soup.

Use a cheese that doesn't get stringy but melts quickly, like jack, fontina, Swiss, Longhorn Cheddar, mild Cheddar, or a process cheese. And you'll need a cracker that won't go limp from the moisture released from the cheese — choose from shredded wheat or thin wheat crackers, Melba toast, crisp rye crackers, or crisp butter crackers.

Place 6 crackers in a circle on a paper plate (make only 6 at a time). Top each cracker with a ¾-inch cube of cheese. Microwave, uncovered, on **HIGH (100%)** for 30 to 45 seconds or until cheese is melted and bubbly. Turn plate, if necessary, after 30 seconds, to cook cheese evenly. Makes 6 snacks.

CHEESEBURGER IN A BUN

For a cheeseburger that's slightly out of the ordinary, smother beef patties with a lightly spiced cheese topping. These burgers can be made ahead and refrigerated — then a quick zap in the microwave and they're ready to serve.

> 1 pound lean ground beef
> 1 tablespoon chopped green onion
> ½ teaspoon salt
> ¼ teaspoon pepper
> 2 tablespoons catsup
> Cheese topping (recipe follows)
> 4 hamburger buns, split and toasted

In a small bowl, combine beef, onion, salt, pepper, and catsup; mix well and shape into 4 equal patties. Arrange in a single layer in a 9-inch baking dish. Cover with wax paper. Microwave on **HIGH (100%)** for 3 minutes. Drain off juices and turn patties over. Microwave, covered, on **HIGH (100%)** for 2 to 4 minutes or until done to your liking. Transfer patties to paper towels to drain; let cool. Prepare cheese topping.

Place each patty on a bun half; cover with about a fourth of the cheese topping and then the remaining bun half. Tightly wrap each bun in plastic wrap and refrigerate until next day.

To reheat, unwrap bun and place in a paper towel. Microwave on **HIGH (100%)** for about 45 seconds *each* (2½ to 3 minutes total for all cheeseburgers) or until meat is heated through and cheese is melted. Makes 4 servings.

Cheese topping.   In a small bowl, combine 1 cup (4 oz.) shredded sharp **Cheddar cheese**, 2 tablespoons **butter** or margarine (softened), 1½ teaspoons **catsup**, 1 teaspoon **prepared mustard**, and 1 tablespoon finely chopped **green onion**.

CHILI BEANS MEXICANA

On a chilly day, this lightly spiced entrée is perfect for lunch or supper with a green salad or fresh fruit. For a heartier meal, tuck it in the microwave first; then while it stands, cook hot dogs to go alongside.

> 1 can (15 oz.) chili beans
> 1 can (12 oz.) whole kernel corn with red and green peppers, drained well
> 1 can (2¼ oz.) sliced ripe olives, drained well
> 1 can (8 oz.) tomato sauce
> 1 tablespoon instant minced onion
> ¼ teaspoon chili powder (optional)
> 2 cups (8 oz.) shredded Cheddar cheese
> 2 cups packaged corn chips

In a 2-quart baking dish, combine chili beans, corn, olives, tomato sauce, onion, chili powder (if used), and 1 cup of the cheese. Coarsely crush 1 cup of the corn chips. Add to bean mixture and stir well. Cover with a lid or plastic wrap. Microwave on **HIGH (100%)** for 7 to 8 minutes (stirring after 4 minutes) or until heated through.

Sprinkle with remaining 1 cup cheese. Cover and let stand for 2 to 3 minutes or until cheese is melted. Place remaining 1 cup corn chips in a circle around the inside of dish. Makes 4 to 6 servings.

S'MORES

Everyone loves these yummy marshmallow and chocolate sandwiches — and they microwave in just seconds. But take care: marshmallows, with their high sugar content, scorch and toughen when overcooked; though we give estimated times, the best doneness test is to watch through the oven door. Remove the cracker just as soon as the marshmallow puffs up and doubles in size.

> 2 graham cracker squares
> ⅓ of a 1.05-ounce milk chocolate bar
> 1 large marshmallow

Place 1 cracker square on a paper towel. Top with chocolate square, then with marshmallow. Microwave, uncovered, on **HIGH (100%)** for 10 to 15 seconds or until marshmallow puffs and doubles in size. Top with remaining cracker and press lightly. Let stand, uncovered, for 1 minute or until chocolate is melted. Makes 1 serving.

For 2 S'mores allow 20 to 25 seconds, for 3 allow 25 to 30 seconds, and for 4 allow 30 to 40 seconds. We do not recommend microwaving more than 4 at a time.

CREAMY DILLED FISH STEAKS

Dill and vermouth accent a creamy sauce enveloping juicy fish steaks.

2 pounds **fish steaks (halibut, swordfish, lingcod, sea bass, or salmon)**, *each* about ¾ inch thick (thawed if frozen)
2 tablespoons **butter or margarine**
¼ teaspoon **dill weed**
1 tablespoon **vermouth**
3 tablespoons **whipping cream**
   Salt and pepper

Pat fish dry. Cut into serving-size pieces. Place butter and dill weed in a 7 by 11-inch baking dish. Microwave, uncovered, on **HIGH (100%)** for 30 seconds or until butter is melted. Stir in vermouth.

Arrange fish in a single layer on bottom of dish; spoon some of the sauce over fish. Cover with wax paper. Microwave on **HIGH (100%)** for 3 minutes. Turn fish over, bringing cooked portions to inside of dish.

Microwave, covered, on **HIGH (100%)** for 5 to 7 minutes or until fish flakes readily when prodded in thickest portion with a fork. Transfer fish to a serving plate. Add cream to drippings, and microwave for 2 to 3 minutes or until mixture begins to boil. Sprinkle with salt and pepper to taste. Spoon sauce over fish. Makes 4 servings.

DILLED TUNA CASSEROLE

Many cooks keep a recipe for tuna-noodle casserole handy and all its ingredients ready and waiting on the pantry shelf. For the cook with a microwave, our version may become just

such a reliable family favorite. Dill weed, celery seeds, and a dash of sherry give this simple casserole its distinctive flavor.

1 tablespoon **butter or margarine**
¼ pound **mushrooms, sliced**
1 cup **frozen peas**
1 can (10¾ oz.) **condensed cream of mushroom soup**
1 tablespoon **dry sherry or milk**
1 can (about 7 oz.) **chunk-style tuna, drained and flaked**
3 ounces **spiral-shaped pasta, cooked and drained**
¼ teaspoon **garlic salt**
¼ teaspoon *each* **celery seeds and dill weed**
   Dash of pepper
½ cup **butter cracker crumbs**

In a 1½-quart casserole, place butter, mushrooms, and peas. Cover with wax paper. Microwave on **HIGH (100%)** for 2 minutes. Stir in soup, sherry, tuna, pasta, garlic salt, celery seeds, dill weed, and pepper; blend well.

Microwave, covered, on **HIGH (100%)** for 6 to 7 minutes (stirring after 4 minutes) or until heated through. Stir well; then sprinkle with cracker crumbs. Microwave, uncovered, on **HIGH (100%)** for 2 minutes. Makes 4 servings.

SCAMPI

Though the large prawns known as *scampi* are actually native Italians that stay close to home, the medium-size shrimp from American waters make perfect substitutes.

Cook the shrimp just until they turn pink — if overcooked, they'll become rubbery. Serve portions with crusty Italian bread, a tossed green salad, and chilled wine.

1 tablespoon **butter or margarine**
1 tablespoon **olive oil or salad oil**
⅓ cup **finely chopped onion**
3 large cloves **garlic, minced or pressed**
1 pound **medium-size raw shrimp (30 to 32 count), shelled and deveined**
2 teaspoons **lemon juice**
3 tablespoons **dry white wine**
3 or 4 drops **liquid hot pepper seasoning**
   Chopped parsley
   Salt and pepper

In a 1½-quart casserole, place butter, oil, onion, and garlic. Microwave, uncovered, on **HIGH (100%)** for 2 minutes.

Stir in shrimp, lemon juice, wine, and hot pepper seasoning. Microwave, uncovered, on **HIGH (100%)** for 4 to 5 minutes (stirring to bring cooked shrimp to inside of dish every 2 minutes) or until pink. Sprinkle with chopped parsley. Season to taste with salt and pepper. Makes 2 servings.

For a kid-pleasing meal, offer a hearty Sloppy-Joe-Topped Potato (recipe on page 57), fresh vegetables, an apple, and a cup of milk. Then watch it disappear.

Vegetables

In vegetable cookery, the microwave oven is truly a wonder worker.

Generally, the secret of success with vegetables is to cook them as briefly as possible, using very little water. And this is exactly what the microwave does: it cooks vegetables in minutes, often without any nutrient-depleting liquid whatsoever. The bonuses to you are garden-fresh flavors and crispness, along with maximum retention of vitamins and minerals.

TIPS & TECHNIQUES

○ **Cutting vegetables.** To assure even cooking, cut vegetables in slices or chunks of uniform size — whether your dish contains only one vegetable or a combination of several.

○ **Adding salt.** If you're using a cooking liquid, add the salt to the liquid; if not, salt the vegetables after they're cooked. Never sprinkle salt directly over vegetables, since salt dehydrates them and interferes with the microwave cooking pattern, leaving dark "freckles" where the salt was sprinkled.

○ **Cooking time.** Check the charts on pages 49–52 to determine which vegetables have the same method and cooking time in common and therefore can be cooked together.

Here's a very general guide for all vegetables. Allow 6 to 7 minutes per pound, and stir or rotate after every 3 minutes, bringing the colder center portions toward the outer edges of the dish. After minimum cooking time, let stand, then check for doneness, since each oven model differs from all the others. Cooking time will also vary slightly depending on the freshness, the moisture content, the maturity, and even the shapes of the vegetables; this is true whether it's vegetables of the same kind, or a combination.

○ **Arranging the vegetables.** Since the woody stems of such vegetables as asparagus and broccoli cook more slowly than the tips or buds, they should be arranged with their stem ends near the outside of the dish and their tips or buds meeting at the center. Halfway through the cooking time, turn the dish and rearrange the vegetables, bringing the center pieces to the outer edge of the dish, to assure even cooking.

Arrange irregularly shaped vegetables such as potatoes and acorn squash with their smaller ends pointing toward the oven center.

Place vegetables you're cooking whole — such as corn, potatoes, and tomatoes — at least 1 inch apart for even cooking. For more on arranging vegetables, consult the placement chart for one to eight items on page 8.

○ **Covering vegetables.** To hold in steam, cover vegetables either with plastic wrap or with the lid of the casserole. In some recipes, we recommend covering with pleated plastic wrap (you'll find folding directions on (page 7). The point is that as steam builds, the pleat unfolds under the pressure; tautly stretched plastic, on the other hand, might split, and the steam would be lost.

Caution: When you uncover a dish after cooking, be careful to start at the edge farthest away from you, since the escaping steam can cause burns.

○ **Using vegetables' natural covering.** Potatoes, squash, and corn on the cob, left whole and unpeeled or unhusked, have a natural covering. Simply pierce the skin of potatoes or squash (corn is all right as it is) with a fork or knife to allow steam to escape, since if left unpierced, the vegetable might explode. Then microwave without using any wrapping other than the natural one.

○ **Standing time.** Vegetables, like other microwaved food, need a brief standing time to finish cooking. Allow from 2 to 5 minutes standing time for vegetables; leaving the cover on, unless otherwise directed in a recipe or in the charts on pages 49–52. If, after standing, vegetables are still too crisp for your liking, cook them further in 1-minute increments. But remember, microwaved vegetables should be crisp-tender; if overcooked, they will dehydrate.

○ **Don't microwave these vegetables.** Dried peas and beans cook to tenderness more effectively in a conventional oven or on a conventional range.

Rice, though not commonly considered a vegetable, is worth a mention here, too. It takes as long to steam rice in a microwave oven as it does on a range. If you need to cook rice quickly, you can substitute instant rice, as we did in our Rice-stuffed Pepper Cups (page 56).

FRESH VEGETABLE COOKING CHART

Cut vegetables in uniform pieces for even cooking. Timing depends on quality and moisture content of vegetables. All vegetables are cooked on **HIGH (100%)**. Use shortest cooking time and allow food to stand for recommended time before microwaving longer; then microwave at 1-minute intervals. Cooked vegetables should be crisp-tender.

Vegetable	Amount (for 4 servings)	Container	Preparation	Cooking Time (CT), Standing Time (ST)	Suggested Seasonings
Artichokes	1 medium (6–8 oz.)	10-oz. custard cup	Remove coarse outer leaves. Trim stem so artichoke will stand upright when served. With a sharp knife, cut off top ⅓ of vegetable. Trim thorn from tip of each leaf. Wash artichoke and turn upside down in container. Pour in ¼ cup water. Cover with pleated plastic wrap (page 7).	CT: 5–7 minutes Before standing, lower leaves should be easy to pull away from stems with a slight tug; stem is fork-tender ST: 5 minutes, covered	Butter, mayonnaise, lemon juice
	2 medium	9" round baking dish	Same as above; use ½ cup water.	CT: 8–10 minutes ST: 5 minutes, covered	Same as above
	3 medium	9" round baking dish	Same as above; use ¾ cup water.	CT: 9–11 minutes ST: 5 minutes, covered	Same as above
	4 medium	9" round baking dish	Same as above; use 1 cup water.	CT: 13–15 minutes ST: 5 minutes, covered	Same as above
Asparagus Spears	1 bunch (1 lb.)	7 by 11" baking dish	Snap off tough ends. Place asparagus so buds are toward center of dish. Add 3 tablespoons water. Cover with pleated plastic wrap (page 7).	CT: 5 minutes Rearrange spears halfway through cooking, bringing center pieces to edge of dish; cover again ST: 5 minutes, covered	Salt and pepper, butter, hollandaise sauce (page 67) cheese sauce

(Continued on next page)

Vegetable	Amount (for 4 servings)	Container	Preparation	Cooking Time (CT), Standing Time (ST)	Suggested Seasonings
Asparagus (cont'd.) Pieces	1 bunch (1 lb.)	1½-qt. casserole	Snap off tough ends. Cut asparagus into 1" pieces. Add 2 tablespoons water. Cover with lid or plastic wrap.	CT: 6–7 minutes Stir after 4 minutes; cover again. ST: 4–5 minutes, covered	Same as above
Beans, green or wax	1 lb.	1½-qt. casserole	Snap off both ends and pull off string. Cut beans into 1" pieces. Add ½ cup water. Cover with lid or plastic wrap.	CT: 12–15 minutes Stir after every 5 minutes ST: 5 minutes, covered Degree of tenderness depends on variety used and maturity of beans	Butter, salt and pepper, minced onion, crumbled bacon, toasted slivered almonds
Bean sprouts	1 lb.	2-qt. casserole	Rinse in cold water just before using. Discard any discolored sprouts; drain. *Do not add water.* Cover with lid or plastic wrap.	CT: 4–5 minutes Stir after 2 minutes ST: 2 minutes, covered	Butter, soy sauce, minced garlic, minced onion
Beets	2 bunches (6 medium)	2-qt. casserole	Cut off green tops about 1" above crown; leave root ends intact. *Do not peel before cooking.* Wash beets. Add 1–1½ cups water. Cover with lid or plastic wrap.	CT: 14–16 minutes Stir after 7 minutes ST: 5 minutes, covered Let cool until easy to handle, then peel	Salt and pepper, butter, lemon juice, wine vinegar
Bok choy (see Swiss chard)					
Broccoli Spears	1 bunch (1¼–1½ lbs.)	9 by 13" baking dish or flat 12" plate	Cut stalks into uniform spears, leaving about 3½" of stalk on each bud. Peel skin off 2" of stalk. Wash broccoli and place so buds are toward center of dish and stalk ends toward outside. *Do not add water.* Cover with pleated plastic wrap (page 7).	CT: 8–10 minutes If using baking dish, rearrange spears halfway through cooking, bringing center pieces to edge of dish. If using plate, just rotate plate ¼ turn ST: 4 minutes, covered	Salt and pepper, butter, mayonnaise, lemon juice, grated Parmesan cheese, cheese sauce
Pieces	1 bunch (1¼–1½ lbs.)	2-qt. casserole	Cut stalks into uniform spears, leaving about 2½" of stalk on each bud. Peel skin off 2" of stalk. Wash broccoli and cut into 1" pieces. Sprinkle with 1 tablespoon water. Cover with lid or plastic wrap.	CT: 5–6 minutes Stir after 3 minutes ST: 4 minutes, covered	Same as above
Brussels sprouts	1 lb. (about 24 medium)	1½-qt. casserole	Cut off stem ends and remove any discolored leaves. If Brussels sprouts are not of uniform size, cut larger ones in half. Add 2 tablespoons water. Cover with lid or plastic wrap.	CT: 6–7 minutes Stir after 3 minutes ST: 3–5 minutes, covered	Salt and pepper, butter, cheese sauce, buttered bread crumbs, grated Parmesan cheese
Cabbage, green or red Shredded	1 lb. (6 cups)	2 to 3-qt. casserole	Discard any wilted outer leaves. Wash and shred cabbage. Add 2 tablespoons water. Cover with lid or plastic wrap.	CT: 4–6 minutes Stir after 4 minutes ST: 3 minutes, covered	Salt and pepper, butter, grated cheese, sour cream
Wedges	1 lb. (small head)	9 to 10" baking dish or pie plate	Discard any wilted outer leaves. Wash and cut into 4 wedges. Arrange wedges like spokes, with large core ends toward edge of dish. Sprinkle with 2 tablespoons water. Cover with lid or pleated plastic wrap (page 7).	CT: 6–8 minutes Rotate dish ¼ turn after 3 minutes ST: 2–3 minutes, covered	Same as above
Napa cabbage (Chinese cabbage)	1 head (1¼–1½ lbs.)	3-qt. casserole	Discard any wilted outer leaves. Wash and cut head in half lengthwise, then cut into 1" pieces. Add 2 tablespoons water. Cover with lid or plastic wrap.	CT: 5–6 minutes Stir after 3 minutes ST: 3 minutes, covered	Salt and pepper, butter, minced onion, cream cheese, chives
Carrots Whole	1 lb. Select carrots about 1 inch in diameter from top to bottom with little tapering at root end.	7 by 11" baking dish	Scrub clean or peel with vegetable peeler; cut off ends. If carrots taper too much on root end, cut off; otherwise ends will cook faster than tops. Add ¼ cup water. Cover with plastic wrap.	CT: 6–7 minutes Rotate each carrot ½ turn after 3 minutes ST: 5 minutes, covered	Salt and pepper, butter, brown sugar, ground ginger, lemon juice, chopped parsley

Vegetable	Amount (for 4 servings)	Container	Preparation	Cooking Time (CT), Standing Time (ST)	Suggested Seasonings
Carrots (cont'd.) Sliced	1 lb. Select carrots about 1 inch in diameter from top to bottom, with little tapering at root end.	1-qt. casserole	Scrub clean or peel with vegetable peeler; cut off ends, then cut carrots into ¼"-thick slices. Add 3 tablespoons water. Cover with lid or plastic wrap.	**CT:** 8–9 minutes Stir after 4 minutes **ST:** 5 minutes, covered	Same as above
Cauliflower Whole	1¼–1½-lb. head (medium)	1-1½ qt. casserole	Remove outer leaves and trim stem so head can stand upright. Wash and place stem side down. Add 2 tablespoons water. Cover with lid or plastic wrap.	**CT:** 10–11 minutes Turn over after 7 minutes; cover again. Before standing, stem end should be fork-tender **ST:** 5 minutes, covered	Salt and pepper, butter, cheese sauce, dill weed, chopped chives
Flowerets	1¼–1½-lb. head (medium)	1½-qt. casserole	Remove outer leaves and trim stem close to base. Break cauliflower into flowerets, and cut larger ones in half. Add 2 tablespoons water. Cover with lid or plastic wrap.	**CT:** 6–8 minutes Stir after 4 minutes; cover again **ST:** 4 minutes, covered	Same as above
Corn on the cob	1–6 ears	None	Be sure corn is completely enclosed in husk, and secure ends with string or rubber bands. (Or remove husk and silk and wrap each ear individually in plastic wrap — makes cooking a little more uniform.) Arrange on paper towels on microwave floor: place 1 ear in center of oven, 2 ears side by side, 3 in triangle, 4 ears in square, 5 ears — place 4 in line and 1 across top, 6 ears — place 4 in line, 1 across top and 1 across bottom.	**CT:** 3–4 minutes per ear Turn each ear over halfway through cooking **ST:** 2–3 minutes	Salt and pepper, seasoned salt, butter
Greens Kale	1 bunch (about 1¼ lbs.)	3-qt. casserole	Rinse and coarsely chop greens. *Do not add water.* Cover with lid or plastic wrap.	**CT:** 7–8 minutes Stir after 3 minutes **ST:** 2 minutes, covered	Salt and pepper, butter crumbled bacon, dill weed, sour cream
Mustard	2 bunches (about 1¼ lbs. total)	3-qt. casserole	Same as above	Same as above	Salt, butter, crumbled bacon, minced onion
Leeks	1½ lbs.	8" square baking dish	Cut off root ends. Trim tops by making a diagonal cut from each side to center point so only about 1¼" of dark green leaves remain. Strip away outer 2 or 3 layers of leaves until you reach non-fibrous interior leaves. Split leeks in half lengthwise. Hold each under running water and separate layers. Arrange in single layer. *Do not add water.* Cover with plastic wrap.	**CT:** 5 minutes **ST:** 5 minutes, covered	Salt and pepper, butter, paprika
Mushrooms	1 lb.	2-qt. casserole	Rinse and pat dry; cut through stem into ¼" slices. Add 2 tablespoons water, or 2 tablespoons butter or margarine cut into 6 pieces. Cover with lid or wax paper.	**CT:** 4–6 minutes Stir after 2 minutes **ST:** 2 minutes, covered	Salt and pepper, butter, minced parsley, tarragon leaves
Onions Quartered	1 lb. (2 large)	1-qt. casserole	Peel and cut into quarters (eighths, if extra large). *Do not add water.* Cover with lid or wax paper.	**CT:** 5–6 minutes Stir after 2 minutes **ST:** 5 minutes, covered	Salt and pepper, butter, paprika
Sliced	1 lb.	1-qt. casserole	Peel onions and cut into ¼"-thick slices. Separate rings. Add 2 tablespoons water, or 2 tablespoons butter or margarine cut into 6 pieces. Cover with lid or wax paper.	**CT:** 5–6 minutes Stir after 2 minutes. (To make onions sweet, cook for 10 minutes, stirring after every 3 minutes) **ST:** 5 minutes, covered	Same as above
Whole (boiling onions)	8–12 onions	1-qt. casserole	Peel. *Do not add water.* Cover with lid or plastic wrap.	**CT:** 4–6 minutes Stir after 2 minutes **ST:** 5 minutes, covered	Same as above

(Continued on next page)

Vegetables **51**

Vegetable	Amount (for 4 servings)	Container	Preparation	Cooking Time (CT), Standing Time (ST)	Suggested Seasonings
Parsnips	1 lb. (4 medium)	1½-qt. casserole	Trim off tops and ends; peel. Cut into ½" cubes. Add ¼ cup water. Cover with lid or plastic wrap.	CT: 8–9 minutes Stir after 4 minutes ST: 5 minutes, covered	Salt and pepper, butter, brown sugar or honey, Worcestershire sauce, lemon juice
Peas Green	About 2½ lbs. (to yield 2½–3 cups, shelled)	1½-qt. casserole	Shell peas and rinse in cold water. Add ¼ cup water. Cover with lid or plastic wrap.	CT: 9–13 minutes Stir after 5 minutes ST: 5 minutes, covered	Salt and pepper, butter, cream sauce, mint, chives, minced onion
Snow (Chinese pea pods)	1 lb.	2-qt. casserole	Snap off both ends and pull off string. Rinse in cold water. *Do not add water.* Cover with lid or plastic wrap.	CT: 4–5 minutes Stir after 2 minutes ST: 4 minutes, covered	Butter, salt, sugar, cream, soy sauce
Potatoes, Baking	1–6 potatoes (8 oz. each)	None	Pierce skin on four sides with fork or knife. Place on paper towels on microwave floor. Arrange as follows, at least 1" apart: 1 potato in center of oven 2 potatoes side by side 3 potatoes in a triangle 4 potatoes in spoke 5 same as above 6 same as above	CT: 4–5 minutes 6–8 minutes 8–10 minutes 10–12 minutes 12–15 minutes 15–20 minutes Turn each potato over halfway through cooking. After cooking, potatoes should give slightly when squeezed. For standing, wrap potatoes in a clean towel or in foil ST: 5–10 minutes, covered	Salt and pepper, butter, sour cream, crumbled bacon, chives, grated Parmesan cheese, cheese sauce
Spinach	1 lb.	3-qt. casserole	Wash leaves and shake off excess moisture. *Do not add water.* Cover with lid or plastic wrap.	CT: 5–7 minutes Stir after 3 minutes ST: 2 minutes, covered	Salt and pepper, butter, crumbled bacon, chopped egg, cream sauce, lemon juice, vinegar
Sweet potatoes (or yams)	1–6 potatoes (about 8 oz. each, fairly round)	None	Prepare and arrange as for baking potatoes (above). 1 sweet potato 2 or 3 sweet potatoes 4 or 5 sweet potatoes 6 sweet potatoes	CT: 4–5 minutes 6–7 minutes 8–10 minutes 10–12 minutes Follow directions given for baking potatoes	Salt and pepper, butter, brown sugar, maple syrup, crushed pineapple
Squash Acorn or Butternut	2 medium (1½ lbs. each)	10–12" flat plate	Wash and pat dry. Cut in half lengthwise and remove seeds. Place squash, hollow side up, on plate with meaty portion toward edge of dish. Cover with plastic wrap.	CT: 10–12 minutes Rotate plate ¼ turn after 5 minutes ST: 5 minutes, covered	Salt and pepper, butter, brown sugar, ground cinnamon, ground nutmeg
Banana	1-lb. slice	7 by 11" baking dish	Rinse and pat dry. Spread cut surface with 1 to 2 tablespoons butter or margarine. Cover with pleated plastic wrap (page 7).	CT: 12–13 minutes Rotate dish ½ turn after 6 minutes. ST: 5 minutes, covered	Same as above
Spaghetti	1 medium (1¼ lbs.)	9 by 13" baking dish	Wash and pat dry. Cut in half lengthwise and remove seeds. Place squash, hollow side up, in dish. Cover with plastic wrap.	CT: 10–12 minutes Rotate each piece ½ turn after 5 minutes; cover again ST: 5 minutes, covered	Same as above
Summer squash (crookneck, pattypan, zucchini)	1 lb.	1½-qt. casserole	Remove ends; wash. Cut squash into ¼" slices. Add 2 tablespoons water, or 2 tablespoons butter or margarine cut into 6 pieces. Cover with lid or plastic wrap.	CT: 6–7 minutes Stir after 3 minutes ST: 3 minutes, covered	Salt and pepper, butter, minced onion, dry beef bouillon, grated Parmesan cheese, tomato sauce
Swiss chard	1 bunch (1¼–1½ lbs.)	2-qt. casserole	Rinse and cut white stems into ¼" pieces and place in casserole with 2 tablespoons water; cover with lid or plastic wrap. Cut leaves into 1" strips to be added after 3 minutes cooking.	CT: 7–8 minutes Stir in leaves after 3 minutes ST: 2 minutes, covered	Salt and pepper, butter, minced onion, crumbled bacon
Turnips	1 lb. (2–3 medium)	1½-qt. casserole	Peel and cut into ½" cubes. Add 3 tablespoons water. Cover with lid or plastic wrap.	CT: 7–9 minutes Stir after 3 minutes; cover again ST: 3 minutes, covered	Salt and pepper, butter, sugar, crumbled bacon, soy sauce, cream sauce

DRESS UP YOUR VEGETABLES

Demure and delicately flavored, vegetables often play second fiddle to their more robust dinner companions. But with a stellar sauce or topping, even the simplest vegetable dish can steal center stage.

Below are some ideas for dramatizing the flavors of a variety of garden favorites. Whether you choose a sauce, seasoned butter, or crisp topper, you'll probably want to keep the entrée fairly simple — roasted or broiled meat, for instance, instead of something with a highly seasoned barbecue sauce.

Quick cheese sauce. In a small bowl, place 1 jar (8 oz.) **process Cheddar cheese** and 1 tablespoon **butter** or margarine. Cover with wax paper. Microwave on **MEDIUM (50%)** for 3 minutes (stirring with a wire whip every minute) or until smooth and heated through.

Serve hot, to spoon over such vegetables as artichokes, asparagus, green beans, broccoli, Brussels sprouts, cauliflower, baked potatoes, and broiled or baked tomatoes. Makes ½ cup.

Sour cream sauce. In a small bowl, place ¼ cup chopped **onion** and 1½ tablespoons **butter** or margarine. Microwave, uncovered, on **HIGH (100%)** for 2 minutes. Stir in 1 tablespoon **all-purpose flour**. Microwave, uncovered, on **HIGH (100%)** for 1 minute. Stir in ½ pint (1 cup) **sour cream**, 1 tablespoon **parsley flakes**, and **salt** to taste. Microwave, uncovered, on **MEDIUM (50%)** for 2 minutes (stirring every minute) or until heated through.

Serve immediately. Or cool, cover, and refrigerate, and serve cold. Either way, this sauce complements such vegetables as asparagus, green beans, broccoli, baked potatoes, broiled or baked tomatoes, and summer squash. Try it over cold vegetables as well. Makes about 1⅓ cups.

Hollandaise sauce. This hot and creamy sauce is delicious spooned over such vegetables as asparagus, green beans, broccoli, Brussels sprouts, green cabbage wedges, cauliflower, and green peas. The recipe is on page 67.

White or dill sauce. Serve this sauce over any hot vegetable, with the exception of yams and yellow squash. The recipe is on page 91.

Spiced butter. In a small bowl, blend ½ cup (¼ lb.) **butter** or margarine (softened), 3 tablespoons firmly packed **brown sugar**, ¼ teaspoon *each* **ground cinnamon** and **allspice**, and ⅛ teaspoon **ground nutmeg**. Cover and refrigerate until needed. Dot over hot vegetables such as sliced beets, carrots, sweet potatoes, any of the yellow squashes, and yams. Makes about ½ cup.

Garlic butter. In a small bowl, place ¼ cup **butter** or margarine. Microwave, uncovered, on **HIGH (100%)** for 1 minute. Stir in 2 cloves **garlic** (minced or pressed) and 1 teaspoon **lemon juice**. Pour over any vegetable of your choice. Or cover and refrigerate; then dot over any hot vegetable. Makes about ¼ cup.

Herb-cheese butter. Use this butter (hot or cold) to season any hot vegetable. The recipe is on page 62.

Crunchy toppers. Sprinkle one or two of these over any cooked vegetable: toasted **nuts** (almonds, pine nuts, pecans, or walnuts), toasted **sesame seeds**, crumbled crisp **bacon**, crushed seasoned **croutons**, crumbled, canned **French fried onions**.

ASPARAGUS AU GRATIN

Tender asparagus slices are baked in a piquant cheese sauce and topped with crisp crumbs — an elegant companion dish for roasted meats or poultry. Or, for a spring brunch, serve the asparagus over toast points or English muffins.

- 1 pound asparagus
- 2 tablespoons water
- 2 tablespoons butter or margarine
- ½ cup *each* finely chopped green pepper and finely chopped onion
- 2 tablespoons all-purpose flour
- ¼ teaspoon salt
  Dash of pepper
- 1 cup milk
- 1½ cups (6 oz.) shredded Cheddar cheese
- ¼ cup crushed croutons

Snap off and discard tough ends of asparagus and cut into 1-inch slanting slices. In a 1½-quart casserole, place asparagus and water. Cover with a lid or plastic wrap. Microwave on **HIGH (100%)** for 6 to 7 minutes (stirring after 4 minutes) or until tender-crisp. Let stand, covered, for 1 minute.

With a slotted spoon, transfer asparagus to a paper towel, reserving juices; set asparagus aside.

Add butter to the reserved juices. Microwave, uncovered, on **HIGH (100%)** for 30 seconds. Stir in green pepper and onion. Microwave, uncovered, on **HIGH (100%)** for 4 minutes, stirring after 2 minutes. Sprinkle with flour, salt, and pepper; mix until blended. Microwave, uncovered, on **HIGH (100%)** for 1 minute or until bubbly.

With a wire whip, beat in milk. Microwave, uncovered, on **HIGH (100%)** for 2 minutes (stirring after 1 minute) or until

bubbly. Stir in cheese, mixing until it is melted; then gently stir in asparagus. Sprinkle with croutons. Microwave, uncovered, on **HIGH (100%)** for 3 minutes, rotating dish ¼ turn after 2 minutes. Makes 4 to 6 servings.

BAKED BEANS SUPREME

Delicious with barbecued hamburgers and hot dogs, this hearty bean casserole is a boon to the busy cook. The microwave cuts conventional baking time in half. If time is short, you can bake the casserole a day ahead.

- ½ pound thinly sliced bacon, diced
- 2 medium-size onions, chopped
- 2 cans (about 1 lb. 4 oz. *each*) pork and beans
- 1½ teaspoons dry mustard
- 1 can (8 oz.) crushed pineapple, drained
- ¼ cup tomato-based chili sauce
- ¼ teaspoon salt

Separate bacon pieces and place over bottom of a 3-quart casserole; cover with a lid or wax paper. Microwave on **HIGH (100%)** for 5 minutes, stirring after 3 minutes. Stir in onions. Microwave, uncovered, on **HIGH (100%)** for 3 minutes or until onions are soft.

Stir in pork and beans, mustard, pineapple, chili sauce, and salt. Cover dish with a lid or plastic wrap. Microwave on

MEDIUM (50%) for 45 minutes, stirring every 15 minutes. Uncover and microwave on **HIGH (100%)** for 10 minutes, stirring every 4 minutes.

If made ahead, cool, cover, and refrigerate until next day. To reheat, microwave, uncovered, on **MEDIUM (50%)** for 12 to 15 minutes (stirring every 5 minutes) or until heated through. Makes 8 to 10 servings.

HARVARD BEETS

Lightly spiced beets make a tangy vegetable treat that's bright with appetizing color. Made from canned beets, this dish will enliven any meal.

- 1 can (1 lb.) diced or sliced beets
- 1 tablespoon cornstarch
- 3 tablespoons sugar
- ¼ teaspoon salt
- 3 tablespoons white vinegar
- 2 whole cloves
- 1 tablespoon butter or margarine

Drain beets, reserving ⅓ cup of the liquid; set aside.

In a 1-quart casserole, combine cornstarch, sugar, and salt. Stir in reserved beet liquid and vinegar. Add beets and cloves; mix gently. Cover with wax paper. Microwave on **HIGH (100%)** for 6 minutes (stirring gently every 2 minutes) or until sauce thickens. Stir in butter. Let stand, covered, for 5 minutes before serving. Makes 4 servings.

ORANGE-GLAZED CARROTS

A tart yet sweet orange glaze adds zest to julienned carrots in this dish — a sure way to win converts to this humble but healthful vegetable.

2 tablespoons sugar
½ teaspoon salt
2 teaspoons cornstarch
⅓ cup orange juice
¾ pound carrots, peeled and cut into 2½-inch julienne strips (to equal 3 cups)

In a small dish, stir together sugar, salt, cornstarch, and 1 tablespoon of the orange juice; set aside.

In a 1½-quart casserole, place carrots and the remaining orange juice. Cover with a lid or plastic wrap. Microwave on **HIGH (100%)** for 6 minutes. Stir cornstarch mixture once, then add to carrots and toss gently. Microwave, uncovered, on **HIGH (100%)** for 2 to 3 minutes (stirring every minute) or until sauce thickens and carrots are fork-tender. Let stand, uncovered, for 5 minutes before serving. Makes 4 servings.

QUICK MEXICAN CORN

Crunchy morsels of green pepper, kernels of sweet corn, and tidbits of pimento combine in this quick and colorful side dish that perks up the appetite with its Latin flavors. Serve alongside hamburgers or baked chicken.

1 large can (about 1 lb.) whole kernel corn, drained well
3 tablespoons finely chopped green pepper
1 tablespoon *each* finely chopped onion and diced pimentos
2 tablespoons butter or margarine

In a 1-quart casserole, combine corn, green pepper, onion, and pimentos; stir to blend. Cut butter into pieces and distribute over corn mixture. Cover with a lid or plastic wrap. Microwave on **HIGH (100%)** for 2 minutes

(stirring after 1 minute) or until heated through. Makes 4 servings.

CREAMY CABBAGE

Cream cheese delicately coats crisp-tender shredded cabbage in this unusual side dish.

6 cups shredded cabbage (about a 1-lb. head)
¼ cup chopped green onions (including tops)
3 tablespoons water
1 small package (3 oz.) cream cheese
½ teaspoon celery seeds
½ teaspoon salt
1 tablespoon butter or margarine

In a 2-quart casserole, place cabbage, onions, and water. Cover with a lid or plastic wrap. Microwave on **HIGH (100%)** for 4 minutes. Stir vegetables. Cut cream cheese into small chunks and add to cabbage mixture, along with celery seeds, salt, and butter. Toss lightly until cheese and butter are melted. Makes 4 servings.

SWEET & SOUR RED CABBAGE

German in origin, this colorful vegetable dish zaps the taste buds with its pungent-sweet flavor. It's a perfect companion for roast game and equally good with hearty sausage.

1½ pounds red cabbage, shredded
1 medium-size tart apple
1 tablespoon butter or margarine
5 tablespoons red wine vinegar
1 teaspoon salt
3 tablespoons sugar

Place cabbage in a 3-quart casserole. Peel, core, and dice

apple. Add to cabbage along with butter and vinegar. Cover with a lid or plastic wrap. Microwave on **HIGH (100%)** for 18 to 22 minutes (stirring every 6 minutes) or until cabbage and apple are tender.

Remove dish from oven using pot holders. Sprinkle with salt and sugar; toss to coat. Microwave, covered, on **HIGH (100%)** for 5 minutes. Let stand, covered, for 5 minutes before serving. Makes 4 to 6 servings.

MUSHROOMS WITH HERBS

Plump mushroom caps become sumptuous bite-size delights when seasoned with aromatic herbs and a sprinkling of sherry. They make a delicious and elegant accompaniment to Fluffy Scrambled Eggs (page 69) and to thick, juicy steaks.

1½ pounds mushrooms, 1 inch in diameter
2 tablespoons butter or margarine
1 tablespoon instant minced onion
1 teaspoon *each* dry basil and oregano leaves
¼ teaspoon *each* thyme leaves, garlic salt, and liquid hot pepper seasoning
1 tablespoon lime juice
2 tablespoons dry sherry

Carefully remove mushroom stems and reserve them for other uses. Set caps aside.

Place butter in a 1½-quart casserole. Microwave, uncovered, on **HIGH (100%)** for 1 minute. Add onion, basil, oregano, thyme, garlic salt, hot pepper seasoning, lime juice, and sherry; mix well. Stir in mushroom caps.

Microwave, uncovered, on **HIGH (100%)** for 5 to 6 minutes (stirring every 2 minutes) or until mushrooms are fork-tender. Makes 4 servings.

RATATOUILLE

A classic summer vegetable casserole from the south of France, ratatouille is as versatile as it is delicious. Serve it hot with meat, or cold as a main dish. Since it gets better as the flavors blend, prepare the dish in advance.

> 4 tablespoons olive oil
> 1 large onion, sliced
> 1 large clove garlic, minced or pressed
> 1 medium-size eggplant (about 1 lb.) peeled and cut into ½-inch cubes
> 3 medium-size zucchini (about 1 lb. total), cut into ¼-inch slices
> 1 large green pepper, seeded and thinly sliced
> 1½ teaspoons dry basil
> ¼ cup minced parsley
> 1 teaspoon salt
> 3 large tomatoes, cut into eighths
> Freshly grated Parmesan cheese (optional)
> Sour cream (optional)

Place oil in a 3-quart casserole. Microwave on **HIGH (100%)** for 1 minute. Stir in onion, garlic, and eggplant. Cover with a lid or plastic wrap. Microwave on **HIGH (100%)** for 3 minutes. Stir in zucchini, green pepper, basil, and parsley. Microwave, covered, on **HIGH (100%)** for 10 minutes, stirring after 5 minutes.

Stir in salt and tomatoes. Microwave, covered, on **HIGH (100%)** for 5 minutes or until vegetables are fork-tender. Let stand, covered, for 10 minutes. Casserole should have a little free liquid, but still be of good spoon-and-serve consistency.

Serve hot, topped with cheese, if desired. Or cool, cover, and refrigerate; serve cold, topping with sour cream, if you wish. Makes 8 to 10 side-dish servings, or 6 main-dish servings.

RICE-STUFFED PEPPER CUPS

For all their festive appearance once they arrive at the table, these tasty stuffed peppers are remarkably quick to prepare.

> 2 large green peppers (¾ to 1 lb. total)
> 2 tablespoons butter or margarine
> 1¼ cups water
> ¼ cup chopped onion
> 1 cup instant long-grain rice
> 1 egg
> ½ teaspoon salt
> Dash of pepper
> 1 small jar (2¼ oz.) diced pimentos, drained
> ½ cup shredded Cheddar cheese

Cut green peppers in half lengthwise and remove stems and seeds. Wash, turn cut side down, and drain well on paper towels; set aside.

In a glass bowl, combine butter, water, onion, and rice. Cover with wax paper. Microwave on **HIGH (100%)** for 2 minutes. Stir rice; cover again with wax paper, and let stand for 5 minutes.

Lightly beat egg and add it to rice mixture along with salt, pepper, pimentos, and cheese; mix well. Mound mixture in green pepper halves and arrange on a flat 10-inch plate. Microwave, uncovered, on **HIGH (100%)** for 8 minutes, rotating each green pepper ½ turn after 4 minutes. Let stand, uncovered, for 5 minutes before serving. Makes 4 servings.

STUFFED POTATOES

(Pictured on front cover)

Baked potatoes are transformed into fluffy, plump, stuffed potatoes laced with Cheddar cheese and chopped green onion, in this delicious vegetable side-dish. A boon to the busy cook, these can be made a day ahead.

> 4 hot baked potatoes (page 52)
> ¼ cup butter or margarine
> ½ cup half-and-half (light cream)
> ½ cup shredded Cheddar cheese
> 2 tablespoons finely chopped green onion (including tops)
> ½ teaspoon salt
> Dash of pepper
> Chopped green onion (optional)
> Paprika (optional)

Cut off a small top section from each potato. Leaving a ¼-inch shell, scoop out potato pulp into a medium-size bowl. To potato pulp add butter, half-and-half, ⅓ cup of the cheese, onion, salt, and pepper; mash with fork or potato masher until well blended. Mound potato mixture into potato shells.

Place stuffed potatoes on a 9-inch pie plate or flat 10-inch plate; cover with plastic wrap. If made ahead, cover and refrigerate until next day.

To serve, microwave, covered, on **HIGH (100%)** for 2 minutes, rotating dish ¼ turn after 1 minute (if refrigerated, microwave for 3½ to 4 minutes, rotating each potato ½ turn after 2 minutes) or until heated through. Sprinkle remaining cheese over potato tops. Garnish with chopped onion or paprika, if desired. Makes 4 servings.

AU GRATIN POTATO RAMEKINS

Clock-conscious cooks will appreciate this easy and flavorful variation on the potato theme. In each individual ramekin, a creamy onion and cheese sauce coats nuggets of the favorite family vegetable.

(Continued on page 59)

BAKED POTATO ENTRÉES

As delicious as they are nutritious, baked potatoes are also thrifty, easy, and surprisingly speedy when cooked in a microwave oven. With all of these benefits, why not make them the focus of a family supper? Rarely, if ever, has a plain-Jane Idaho experienced such elegance of dress — in the recipes below we present potatoes with two different savory toppings. Each person can add further glory to their entrée by embellishing it with tasty garnishes. Add a crisp, vinaigrette-dressed salad and you have a simple but splendid meal.

HAM & CHEESE-STACKED POTATOES

Ham and cheese only begin the taste experience of these super baked potatoes. With a dollop of each of the five condiments, the potatoes can become as elaborate as Dagwood's sandwiches.

    6 strips bacon, cooked and crumbled
    1 large tomato, diced
    ½ avocado, diced and tossed with
        1 teaspoon lemon juice
    ½ to 1 cup sour cream
    ½ cup chopped green onions
        (including tops)
    4 hot baked potatoes (page 52)
    4 tablespoons butter or margarine
    1⅓ cups (about 5 oz.) shredded
        Cheddar cheese
    1 cup diced cooked ham

Place bacon, tomato, avocado, sour cream, and onions in individual bowls to serve as condiments.

Make a cross slit in each potato top. With both hands, gently squeeze potato on each end, slightly pushing meaty potato pulp up through top. Arrange potatoes on individual serving plates. Place 1 tablespoon of the butter in each potato opening, then ⅓ cup of the cheese, and ¼ cup of the ham. At the table, pass bowls of condiments. Makes 4 servings.

SLOPPY-JOE-TOPPED POTATOES

(Pictured on page 47)

Cool-weather appetites call for hearty potato toppings. Here's one to win everyone over — a rich meat and tomato sauce lightly spiced with chili powder.

    1 pound lean ground beef
    ¾ cup *each* chopped celery and
        chopped onion
    1 clove garlic, minced or pressed
    1 can (about 1 lb.) whole tomatoes
    1 can (6 oz.) tomato paste
    1 teaspoon salt
    2½ teaspoons chili powder
    6 hot baked potatoes (page 52)
    1 cup (4 oz.) shredded Cheddar cheese
    ½ pint (1 cup) sour cream

In a 2-quart casserole, place beef, breaking it up with a fork. Microwave, uncovered, on **HIGH (100%)** for 2½ minutes. Drain off fat and break up large pieces. Add celery, onion, and garlic. Cover with wax paper. Microwave on **HIGH (100%)** for 4 minutes, stirring after 2 minutes. Drain off fat.

Add tomatoes (break up with a spoon) and their liquid, tomato paste, salt, and chili powder. Cover with a lid or plastic wrap. Microwave on **MEDIUM (50%)** for 15 minutes (stirring every 5 minutes) or until sauce has thickened and mixture is heated through.

If made ahead, cool, cover, and refrigerate until next day. To reheat, microwave on **HIGH (100%)** for 4 to 6 minutes (stirring every 2 minutes) or until heated through.

Make a cross slit in each potato top. With both hands, gently squeeze potato on each end, slightly pushing meaty potato pulp up through top. Arrange potatoes on individual serving plates. Ladle about 1 cup of the tomato-beef mixture over each potato. Pass cheese and sour cream at the table. Makes 6 servings.

Vegetables **57**

Butter or margarine

4 russet potatoes (2 lbs. total),
peeled and cubed

4 teaspoons instant minced
onion

2 teaspoons salt

4 tablespoons firm butter or
margarine, cut into pieces

½ pint (1 cup) whipping
cream or half-and-half
(light cream)

1 cup (4 oz.) shredded
Swiss cheese

Generously butter four 10-ounce ramekins or custard cups. Arrange potato cubes in ramekins. Sprinkle each with 1 teaspoon of the onion and ½ teaspoon of the salt. Evenly dot ramekins with butter pieces. Pour ¼ cup of the cream over each ramekin, then sprinkle each with ¼ cup of the cheese.

Cover each ramekin with pleated plastic wrap (page 7). Arrange in a circle on a flat 12-inch plate. Microwave on **HIGH (100%)** for 10 minutes, rotating plate ¼ turn after 5 minutes.

Starting at far edge of one ramekin, carefully fold back plastic wrap. Potatoes should be fork-tender. If undercooked, microwave on **HIGH (100%)** for 1 to 2 more minutes or until fork-tender. Let stand, covered, for 5 minutes. Makes 4 servings.

MEXICAN ZUCCHINI CASSEROLE

Colorful and zesty, this zucchini casserole makes an impressive accompaniment to any main dish. For even cooking, choose zucchini of uniform widths.

Shapely acorn squash halves become edible bowls for a rich, sweet filling of blueberries and apples. Hearty fare, they round out a meal served alongside a simple entrée of poultry or meat. The recipe for Acorn Squash with Fruit is on this page.

3 medium-size zucchini (about
1 lb. total), cut into ⅛-inch
slices

1 can (8 oz.) tomato sauce

½ to 1 can (4 oz.) green chili
peppers, seeded and
chopped

3 tablespoons thinly sliced
green onions (including tops)

¼ teaspoon ground cumin

1 can (2¼ oz.) sliced ripe
olives, drained well

1 cup (4 oz.) shredded
Cheddar cheese

About ½ cup sour cream
(optional)

Place zucchini in a 1½-quart casserole, cover with a lid or plastic wrap. Microwave on **HIGH (100%)** for 3 minutes; stir vegetables, and drain off liquid.

In a medium-size bowl, combine tomato sauce, chili peppers, onions, cumin, and olives. Add to zucchini and stir to blend. Microwave, covered, on **HIGH (100%)** for 5 minutes. Sprinkle with cheese. Microwave, uncovered, on **HIGH (100%)** for 1 minute or until cheese is melted. Pass sour cream at the table, if desired. Makes 4 to 6 servings.

ACORN SQUASH WITH FRUIT

(Pictured on opposite page)

A favorite way of enhancing the subtle flavor of winter squash is to sweeten its meat; in this version, a blueberry-apple filling adds a touch of sweetness and creates a colorful work of art.

2 acorn squash (about 3 lbs. total)

¼ cup firmly packed brown sugar

¾ teaspoon ground cinnamon

1 teaspoon cornstarch

¼ teaspoon salt

1 cup frozen blueberries, thawed
and drained well

¾ cup finely diced apple

1 tablespoon butter or margarine
Salt

Cut squash in half lengthwise and remove seeds. Place squash, hollow side up, on a flat 12-inch plate, with stem ends to outside of dish. Cover with plastic wrap. Microwave on **HIGH (100%)** for 10 minutes, rotating dish ¼ turn after 5 minutes.

Starting at far edge, carefully fold back plastic wrap; squash should be fork-tender when pierced on top surface (do *not* pierce through skin). If undercooked, microwave on **HIGH (100%)** for 1 to 2 more minutes. Let stand, covered, while preparing fruit.

In a small bowl, combine brown sugar, cinnamon, cornstarch, and the ¼ teaspoon salt; blend well. Stir in blueberries and apple pieces. Microwave, uncovered, on **HIGH (100%)** for 4 minutes (stirring after 2 minutes) or until sauce is slightly thickened. Stir in butter.

Lightly salt each squash cavity and fill with blueberry-apple sauce. Makes 4 servings.

SEASONED GREEN PEAS

For unexpected company or a quick family side dish, this simple herbed vegetable goes from freezer to table in minutes.

1 package (10 oz.) frozen tiny peas

1 teaspoon instant minced onion

¼ teaspoon thyme leaves

2 tablespoons firm butter
or margarine, cut into
4 pieces

Salt and pepper to taste

In a 1-quart casserole with a lid, place peas, breaking them up as much as possible. Sprinkle with onion and thyme. Dot with butter. Microwave, covered, on **HIGH (100%)** for 4 to 5 minutes (stirring after 3 minutes) or until heated through. Let stand, covered, for 2 minutes. Makes 4 servings.

For a quick and complete meal, serve any of these soups with thick wedges of cheese, crisp lettuce leaves, and chunks of French bread.

SWEET & SOUR BEAN SOUP

So mellow and satisfying, this soup tastes as if it simmered all day on the back of the stove. It's hard to believe that you can whip it together with pantry shelf canned goods. Keep it in mind for rescue on busy days — as well as for comfort on wintry ones.

    8   strips thinly sliced bacon, diced
    1   small onion, chopped
    1   clove garlic, minced or pressed
    1   can (about 16 oz.) stewed tomatoes
    2   cans (about 1 lb. *each*) red kidney beans
    1   teaspoon chili powder
    ¼   teaspoon *each* thyme leaves and dry basil
    2   tablespoons red wine vinegar
        Sour cream (optional)

Separate bacon pieces and place over bottom of a 3-quart casserole or soup tureen. Cover with a lid or wax paper. Microwave on **HIGH (100%)** for 5 minutes, stirring after 3 minutes. With a slotted spoon, lift out bacon and drain on paper towels.

Discard all but 2 tablespoons of the drippings.

To drippings add onion and garlic. Microwave, covered, on **HIGH (100%)** for 4 minutes, stirring after 2 minutes. Add tomatoes and their liquid. Reserving 1 cup of the beans, place remaining beans and their liquid in casserole. Mash reserved beans with a fork and add to casserole along with chili powder, thyme, and basil.

Microwave, covered, on **HIGH (100%)** for 8 to 10 minutes (stirring after 4 minutes) or until piping hot. Stir in vinegar and bacon. Pass a bowl of sour cream at the table, if desired. Makes 4 to 6 servings.

CLAM & CORN CHOWDER

For those busy days when the clock seems to race ahead of you, this creamy chowder makes an easy and delicious lunch or light supper entrée. Serve it with a green salad and crisp crackers.

    2   tablespoons butter or margarine
    1   small onion, chopped
    2   cans (6½ oz. *each*) chopped clams
    1   bottle (8 oz.) clam juice
    1   can (17 oz.) cream-style corn
    1   cup milk
    ¼   teaspoon liquid hot pepper seasoning
        Condiments: About ½ cup *each* chopped hard-cooked egg, crumbled crisp bacon, hulled sunflower seeds, and seasoned croutons

Place butter and onion in a 3-quart casserole. Microwave, uncovered. on **HIGH (100%)** for 4 minutes. Stir in clams and their liquid, clam juice, corn, milk, and hot pepper seasoning. Cover with a lid or plastic wrap. Microwave on **HIGH (100%)** for 7 to 9 minutes (stirring after 4 minutes) or until chowder is steaming. Ladle soup into bowls or mugs. Serve condiments in separate bowls at the table. Makes 7 cups.

MUSHROOM VELVET SOUP

Whether served at a simple picnic or an elegant dinner party, this creamy mushroom soup makes a memorable first course. Offer it chilled or hot, depending on the weather.

½ cup butter or margarine
½ pound mushrooms, sliced
1 medium-size onion, chopped
½ cup chopped parsley, lightly packed
1 tablespoon all-purpose flour
1 can (about 14 oz.) beef broth
½ pint (1 cup) sour cream

Place butter in a 1½-quart casserole. Microwave, uncovered, on **HIGH (100%)** for 30 seconds. Stir in mushrooms, onion, and parsley. Microwave, uncovered, on **HIGH (100%)** for 5 minutes, stirring after 3 minutes. Sprinkle with flour, then stir in ½ cup of the broth. Microwave, uncovered, on **HIGH (100%)** for 1 minute or until bubbly.

In a blender or food processor, whirl vegetable mixture, a portion at a time, with sour cream and remaining broth until smooth.

If made ahead, cool, cover, and refrigerate until next day. Serve cold. Or cover with wax paper and microwave on **MEDIUM (50%)** for 3 minutes (stirring after 1½ minutes) or until heated through. Makes 4 to 6 servings.

FRENCH ONION SOUP

The classic onion soup called "Les Halles" is named for the famous Paris market. Our version uses the traditional ingredients of rich beef broth, thickened with sweet onions and topped with crusty French bread and melted cheese — but the microwave reduces the cooking time by half.

3 large yellow onions, thinly sliced
4 tablespoons firm butter or margarine
2 teaspoons all-purpose flour
6 cups regular-strength beef broth or 6 beef bouillon cubes and 6 cups water
⅓ cup dry white wine
Garlic powder
6 to 8 slices crusty French bread (*each* ½ inch thick), toasted and buttered
1 cup (4 oz.) shredded Swiss cheese

Place onions in a 3-quart casserole or soup tureen. Cut butter into pieces and distribute over onions. Cover with a lid or wax paper. Microwave on **HIGH (100%)** for 15 minutes, stirring every 5 minutes. Stir in flour and microwave, uncovered, on **HIGH (100%)** for 1 minute. Add broth and wine. (At this point you may cover and refrigerate until next day.)

Microwave, covered, on **HIGH (100%)** for 8 minutes (15 to 18 minutes, if refrigerated), stirring every 4 minutes.

To serve, lightly sprinkle garlic powder on hot buttered toast. Place 1 toast slice in each soup bowl; ladle soup over toast. Cover toast generously with cheese. Place 2 or 3 bowls at a time in microwave. Microwave, uncovered, on **HIGH (100%)** for 1½ to 2 minutes or until cheese is melted. Makes 6 to 8 servings.

FRENCH COUNTRY VEGETABLE SOUP

In minutes, you can create the same hearty winter soup that traditionally simmers for hours in a cast iron kettle on French country stoves.

2 tablespoons butter or margarine
2 bunches green onions (including tops), thinly sliced
1 small onion, sliced
1 cup chopped celery
1 large carrot, shredded (to equal 1 cup)
1 medium-size turnip, peeled and cubed
1 large potato, peeled and cubed
2 cans (about 14 oz. *each*) chicken broth
¼ teaspoon marjoram leaves
Salt and pepper

Place butter in a 3-quart casserole or soup tureen. Microwave, uncovered, on **HIGH (100%)** for 30 seconds. Stir in green onions, onion, celery, and carrot. Cover with a lid or plastic wrap. Microwave on **HIGH (100%)** for 10 minutes, stirring after 5 minutes.

Mix in turnip, potato, and ¼ cup of the broth. Microwave, covered, on **HIGH (100%)** for 12 minutes (stirring every 4 minutes) or until potato is fork-tender. Add remaining broth and marjoram.

In a blender or food processor, whirl mixture, a portion at a time, until puréed. Transfer to a tureen or serving bowl. Season with salt and pepper. Microwave, covered, on **HIGH (100%)** for 5 minutes to heat. Makes 4 to 6 servings.

TOMATOES PARMESAN

Tomato halves crowned with a Parmesan-garlic mixture make a colorful accompaniment to fish, meat, or egg entreés.

- 2 firm ripe tomatoes, about 2½ inches in diameter
- 2 tablespoons grated Parmesan cheese
- 1 tablespoon dry bread crumbs
- ½ teaspoon dry basil
- ¼ teaspoon garlic salt
- ⅛ teaspoon garlic powder

Cut each tomato in half horizontally. Arrange in a circle on a flat 10-inch plate.

In a small bowl, stir together cheese, bread crumbs, basil, garlic salt, and garlic powder. Sprinkle mixture evenly over tomato halves.

Microwave, uncovered, on **HIGH (100%)** for 3 minutes, rotating each tomato ½ turn after 1½ minutes. Let stand, uncovered, for 3 to 4 minutes before serving. Makes 2 to 4 servings.

ORIENTAL MEDLEY

We named this dish for its distinctively Oriental flavor, as well as for the typical crunch of tender-crisp vegetables that cook in minutes. Ordinarily, the mélange of greens and mushrooms would be tossed in a wok — but you can get the same results in your microwave.

- ¼ pound bean sprouts, washed and drained well
- ¼ pound mushrooms, cut into ¼-inch slices
- ¼ pound snow peas, ends and strings removed
- 2 green onions (including tops), cut into ¼-inch diagonal slices
- 2 tablespoons peanut oil
- 1 tablespoon soy sauce

In a 2-quart casserole, combine bean sprouts, mushrooms, and snow peas. Cover with a lid or plastic wrap. Microwave on **HIGH (100%)** for 4 minutes; drain off excess water. Add onions. Drizzle oil and soy over vegetables and toss to coat. Serve hot, or refrigerate and serve cold. Makes 4 to 6 servings.

VEGETABLE PLATTER WITH HERB-CHEESE BUTTER

(Pictured on opposite page)

This impressive array of vegetables not only tastes delicious but looks beautiful as a buffet centerpiece. We selected broccoli, cauliflower, and carrots as the main ingredients, because they cook in about the same length of time. For best results, be sure to place each vegetable as indicated.

The broccoli and cauliflower pieces ring the center because they cook quickly. The carrots, a more woody vegetable, point toward the outside rim of the dish. Mushrooms, which cook the fastest, are added toward the end of the cooking time to round out the platter.

After the vegetables are cooked, you set a cup of herb and cheese-flavored butter in the center.

- Herb-cheese butter (recipe follows)
- ½ bunch broccoli (about ¾ lb.), cut into 2½-inch flowerets (peel 2 inches of skin off stalks)
- ½ head cauliflower, cut into flowerets
- 2 to 3 carrots (1 inch in diameter), cut in half lengthwise, then cut into 2-inch lengths
- 2 tablespoons water
- 10 to 12 mushrooms (1 inch in diameter), fluted

Prepare herb-cheese butter.

Place a 10-ounce custard cup in center of a flat 12-inch plate. Place broccoli heads up against custard cup (stalks toward outer edge) in a circle. Place cauliflower on plate next to broccoli heads, forming a circle. Arrange carrot sticks around rim, parallel to broccoli stems.

Sprinkle water over vegetables. Cover with two pieces of plastic wrap, making sure dish is completely covered. Microwave on **HIGH (100%)** for 4 minutes, rotating dish ¼ turn after 2 minutes.

Starting at far edge, carefully remove plastic wrap. Place mushrooms around platter next to carrots. Microwave, covered, on **HIGH (100%)** for 3 more minutes. Let stand, covered, for 2 minutes before serving.

Remove empty custard cup and replace it with herb-cheese butter to be spooned over vegetables. The steam from the hot vegetables melts the butter. Makes about 6 servings.

Herb-cheese butter. In a small bowl, place 6 tablespoons **butter** or margarine, softened; 2 teaspoons **parsley flakes**; ½ teaspoon **Italian herb seasoning**; ¼ teaspoon **garlic salt**; ⅛ teaspoon **pepper**; and 2 to 3 tablespoons grated **Parmesan cheese**; mix well. Transfer to a 10-ounce custard cup, cover, and refrigerate. Makes about ½ cup.

Wreathed around a bowl of rich herb-cheese butter is a colorful medley of vegetables cooked to crisp perfection in the microwave. This Vegetable Platter (recipe at left) is a beautiful appetizer or buffet offering.

Eggs & Cheese

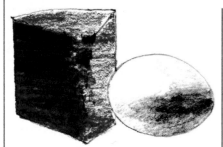

These rich sources of protein make wonderful entrées for any meal of the day — from breakfast right on through lunch, dinner, or a late-night snack.

Eggs and cheese have their idiosyncracies, though, and they are easily made tough by improper cooking, whether it's microwave or conventional. Here are some rules to guide you to superb results as you combine the versatility of eggs and cheese with the convenience and speed of microwave cooking.

TIPS & TECHNIQUES

○ **Unbreakable rule.** The most important lesson — one you don't want to learn the hard way — is this: *Never cook an egg in its shell in the microwave oven.* As the egg cooks, pressure builds up rapidly inside the shell until the egg actually explodes, causing a terrible mess all over your mi-

crowave. So leave soft or hard-cooked eggs for top of the range cooking.

○ **Bring eggs to room temperature.** Eggs will cook more evenly, with fluffier results, if you start with them at room temperature. Instead of waiting the 20 minutes or so that it takes for refrigerated eggs to lose their chill, you can put them into a bowl of lukewarm water and let them stand for a few minutes before you start a recipe. This will bring the eggs at least close to room temperature.

○ **Pricking the egg yolk.** In conventional frying, poaching, or baking, the white of the egg cooks more quickly than the yolk, but in microwave cooking, just the opposite is true. Because of its higher fat content, the yolk attracts more microwaves and consequently cooks faster than the surrounding white.

Before cooking, you need to

prick the membrane that covers the yolk — do this with a fork, penetrating barely beneath the surface; this will allow steam to escape. Otherwise, the egg would very likely explode, just as it would if left in its shell.

○ **Cook eggs covered.** We recommend covering all eggs, except scrambled eggs. The purpose is to protect against splattering as well as to distribute the heat more evenly. You can use wax paper or plastic wrap, as recommended in the recipes in this chapter.

○ **Standing time for eggs.** Always remove egg dishes from the microwave oven while the eggs are still moist — they'll continue to cook upon standing and will set after a few minutes. Eggs left in the microwave too long become disappointingly tough and rubbery. Allow 1 to 4 minutes standing time; if they're still too moist for your liking, microwave them on **HIGH (100%)**, checking at 30-second intervals.

○ **Cheese and the microwave.** Cooking time is as crucial with cheese as it is with eggs. Overcooked cheese can be tough and stringy, even grainy. Here are ways to prevent that.

If a recipe calls for a topping of cheese, add it just before the dish is done, and then microwave 30 seconds to 1 minute; we use this technique for our Baked Eggs in Hash (this page). Or you can sprinkle on the topping as soon as you take the dish from the oven, as in Chili & Cheese Enchiladas (page 68). If the food is hot enough, the heat from the cooked food melts the cheese almost instantly.

Shredded cheese fares better than the strips or chunks that are used in many traditional dishes. An example is our Chili Relleno Casserole (page 68), in which we stuff the chili peppers with shredded cheese for more even melting.

BASIC PUFFY OMELET

Because the classic plain French omelet needs top-of-the-range heat to cook, it can't be microwaved. But a puffy omelet, which finishes cooking in the oven, can easily be converted for the microwave.

For many omelet lovers, the best part is what's hidden inside, so we've listed a number of fillings for this light and airy star attraction of the brunch table.

> 2 eggs, separated
> Dash of salt
> 1 tablespoon half-and-half (light cream)
> 1 tablespoon butter or margarine
> Fillings (suggestions follow)

In a medium-size bowl, beat egg whites and salt until soft, moist peaks form.

In another bowl, combine half-and-half and egg yolks. Using the same beater, beat until thickened; pour over egg whites and gently fold together.

Place butter in a 9-inch pie plate. Microwave, uncovered, on **HIGH (100%)** for 1 minute. Pour in egg mixture, spreading it out to cover bottom of plate. Microwave, uncovered, on **MEDIUM (50%)** for 4 minutes, rotating dish ¼ turn after 2 minutes.

Microwave on **HIGH (100%)** for 30 to 45 seconds or until center does not jiggle when plate is gently shaken. Spoon ¼ to ⅓ cup filling over half the omelet; run a spatula around edge, fold omelet in half, and slide out onto a serving plate. Makes 1 serving.

Fillings. Use alone or in combination: **shredded cheese** (jack, Cheddar, or Parmesan), thinly sliced **spinach**, chopped **green pepper**, chopped **green**

onions or chives, diced **avocado**, sliced **mushrooms** (raw or browned in butter), crumbled crisp **bacon**, diced **salami** or ham, diced **tomato**, small cooked **shrimp, jelly, powdered sugar, sour cream, cream cheese.**

BAKED EGGS IN HASH

For a dramatic presentation, try these eggs baked in individual nests of corned beef hash. Fresh fruit adds a perfect touch of color and contrast to this hearty breakfast for two.

> 1 can (about 15 oz.) corned beef hash
> 2 eggs
> 2 tablespoons shredded sharp Cheddar cheese

Spoon hash evenly into two 10-ounce custard cups or ramekins. With the back of a spoon, make a hollow in center of each, leaving a ¼-inch rim. Carefully crack egg into each hollow. With a fork, prick egg yolks through membrane two times (prevents bursting). Cover with plastic wrap.

Microwave on **HIGH (100%)** for 4 minutes (rotating cups ¼ turn after 2 minutes) or until hash is heated through and egg whites are nearly opaque. Starting at far edge of each cup, carefully remove plastic wrap. Sprinkle each yolk with 1 table-

(Continued on page 67)

spoon of the cheese. Microwave, uncovered, on **HIGH (100%)** for 30 seconds. Let stand for 1 minute before serving. Makes 2 servings.

EGGS BENEDICT

(Pictured on opposite page)

In many an egg-lover's view, this classic of the Sunday brunch (not to mention break-fast in bed) is truly fit for a king. The secret is undoubtedly the hollandaise sauce — it abso-lutely glorifies a little poached egg, and works wonders on the bacon and muffin as well.

- 4 slices Canadian bacon or boneless cooked ham, sliced ⅛ to ¼ inch thick
- 4 English muffins, split
  Butter or margarine
  Hollandaise sauce (recipe follows)
- 4 poached eggs (page 69)

In a wide frying pan over me-dium heat, cook bacon until lightly browned on both sides (about 1 minute on each side). Toast muffin halves and spread with butter. Prepare hollandaise sauce; cover to keep warm while poaching eggs.

To serve, place 1 or 2 muffin halves on each serving plate. Cover one muffin half with ba-con. With a slotted spoon, lift eggs from water, drain briefly, and arrange 1 egg over each bacon-topped muffin. Spoon hollandaise over each egg. Makes 4 servings.

Hollandaise sauce. In a 2-cup glass measure, place ¼ cup **butter** (do *not* use margarine — it separates).

Elegant champagne garden brunch awaits four special people. They'll enjoy Eggs Benedict (recipe above), fruit of the season, and, for a sweet conclusion, Sour Cream Coffee Cake (recipe on page 75).

Microwave, uncovered, on **HIGH (100%)** for 1 minute or until melted. Add 2 **egg yolks**, 2 teaspoons **lemon juice**, ¼ cup **half-and-half** (light cream), ¼ teaspoon **dry mustard**, and a dash of **salt**; beat well with a wire whip.

Microwave, uncovered, on **HIGH (100%)** for 2 minutes (stir-ring after 1 minute, then at 30-second intervals) or until sauce is slightly thickened. Makes about ½ cup.

EGG & HAM SCRAMBLE

Ham and cheese add bold fla-vors to fluffy scrambled eggs in a dish that's ready almost in-stantly. To round out a hearty breakfast, offer Ready-Bake Bran Muffins (page 75) and fresh fruit of the season.

- 1 tablespoon butter or margarine
- 4 eggs
- ¼ cup milk
- ⅛ teaspoon salt
  Dash of pepper
- ¼ cup finely minced cooked ham
- ½ cup shredded Cheddar cheese

Place butter in a shallow 1-quart baking dish. Micro-wave, uncovered, on **HIGH (100%)** for 30 seconds. Crack eggs into a dish. Add milk, salt, and pepper. With a wire whip, beat until well blended.

Microwave, uncovered, on **HIGH (100%)** for 1 minute. Stir in ham and ¼ cup of the cheese. Microwave, uncovered, on **HIGH (100%)** for 2 minutes. Stir, bringing cooked portion to in-side of dish. Sprinkle with re-maining ¼ cup cheese and microwave uncovered on **HIGH (100%)** for 30 more seconds. Let stand for 1 minute before serv-ing. Makes 2 or 3 servings.

EGG SALAD FILLING

This egg concoction is so de-licious that lunch bag carriers in your family will request it in their sandwiches again and again.

Try it with other edible plat-ters, too, for exciting combina-tions of flavor and texture. Spread it on leaves of romaine lettuce, or spoon it into "cups" of tomato, green pepper, or cooked summer squash. Or pair it with celery for a lovely, low-calorie, nutritious snack.

- 1 tablespoon butter or margarine
- 4 eggs
- 3 tablespoons sweet pickle relish
- 2 tablespoons chopped green onion (including top), chopped green pepper, or chopped celery
- 1 teaspoon prepared mustard
- 2 to 3 tablespoons mayonnaise
- ¼ teaspoon salt
  Dash of pepper

Place butter in a 1-quart cas-serole. Microwave, uncovered, on **HIGH (100%)** for 30 seconds. Crack eggs into the dish and thoroughly beat with a fork. Microwave, uncovered, on **HIGH (100%)** for 2 to 2½ minutes, stirring to bring cooked portion to inside of dish after every minute. Eggs should be moist and not completely set. Let stand, uncovered, for 1 minute.

Cover dish with wax paper and refrigerate for 20 minutes (stirring once) or until cool to the touch. (Or place in freezer for 10 minutes, stirring once.)

Add relish, onion, mustard, mayonnaise, and salt; mash with a fork or potato masher until well blended. Season to taste with pepper. Cover and refrigerate until needed. Use within 3 days. Makes about 1½ cups.

CHILI & CHEESE ENCHILADAS

A sauce blended from sour cream and cottage cheese cools the chili bite in these enchiladas. For a festive south-of-the-border repast, serve them with Spanish rice and a tossed green salad. Flaming Bananas Guadalajara (page 89) makes a sweet finale.

½ pint (1 cup) *each* sour cream and small curd cottage cheese
½ envelope (2 tablespoons) dry onion soup mix (amount for 3 or 4 servings)
½ cup chopped green onions (including tops)
2 cans (10 oz. *each*) enchilada sauce
8 corn tortillas (about 7-inch size)
1 can (4 oz.) whole green chili peppers, seeded and cut into 16 strips
2 cups (8 oz.) shredded jack cheese

In a small bowl, stir together sour cream, cottage cheese, onion soup mix, and green onions; blend well and set aside.

Pour ½ cup of the enchilada sauce over bottom of a 7 by 11-inch baking dish; set aside.

Stack tortillas together and wrap in two paper towels. Microwave on **HIGH (100%)** for 1 minute or until tortillas are softened (they roll more easily when soft). Be sure not to over-heat — they become brittle.

To assemble enchiladas, place 1 chili pepper strip down center of each tortilla. Top with 3 tablespoons of the sour cream mixture, then sprinkle with 2 tablespoons of the jack cheese; cover with another chili pepper strip. Roll to enclose. Arrange, seam side down, in sauce in baking dish. Pour remaining enchilada sauce evenly over tortillas. Cover loosely with plastic wrap.

Microwave on **HIGH (100%)** for 10 to 12 minutes (rotating dish ¼ turn after 5 minutes) or until heated through. Sprinkle with remaining 1 cup jack cheese and let stand, covered, for 5 minutes before serving. Makes 8 enchiladas (4 servings).

CREAMY SCRAMBLED EGGS

Sour cream stirred through these scrambled eggs makes them marvelously moist and creamy. For a light brunch or supper, round out the menu with Tomatoes Parmesan (page 62).

2 tablespoons butter or margarine
2 teaspoons all-purpose flour
⅓ cup sour cream
8 eggs
¼ teaspoon salt
⅛ teaspoon white pepper
Chopped parsley

In a 10-ounce custard cup or bowl, place 1 tablespoon of the butter. Microwave, uncovered, on **HIGH (100%)** for 30 seconds. Stir in flour, then sour cream. Microwave, uncovered, on **MEDIUM (50%)** for 1 minute; stir and set aside.

In a 1½-quart casserole, place remaining 1 tablespoon butter. Microwave, uncovered, on **HIGH (100%)** for 30 seconds. Crack eggs into the dish. Add salt and pepper. With a wire whip, beat until well blended. Microwave, uncovered, on **HIGH (100%)** for 4 to 5 minutes, stirring to bring cooked portion to inside of dish after every minute. Eggs should be moist and not completely set.

Stir in sour cream mixture. Sprinkle with parsley and let stand, uncovered, for 1 to 3 minutes before serving. Makes 4 servings.

CHILI RELLENO CASSEROLE

Mild jack cheese and a tomato-herb sauce lend mellow contrast to the peppy Mexican flavors in this chili casserole. Be sure to shred the cheese, rather than simply cutting it into chunks, so it will melt very quickly.

2 cans (4 oz. *each*) whole green chili peppers
2 cups (8 oz.) shredded jack cheese
4 eggs
1 cup milk
¼ cup all-purpose flour
1 teaspoon salt
1 teaspoon instant minced onion
¾ cup shredded Cheddar cheese
Tomato-herb sauce (recipe follows)

Rinse and carefully seed chili peppers, trying to maintain shape. Stuff jack cheese into each chili pepper. Arrange in a 10-inch round baking dish.

In a small bowl, lightly beat eggs with a wire whip. Beat in milk, flour, salt, and onion; pour over chili peppers. Cover with wax paper. Microwave on **MEDIUM (50%)** for 10 minutes, rotating dish ¼ turn after 5 minutes. Uncover and microwave on **HIGH (100%)** for 3 to 5 minutes (rotating dish ¼ turn after every 1½ minutes) or until center jiggles slightly when dish is gently shaken. (Upon standing, center will set.)

Sprinkle with Cheddar cheese and let stand for 10 minutes before serving. Meanwhile, prepare tomato-herb sauce; pass at the table to spoon over individual servings. Makes about 6 servings.

Tomato-herb sauce. In a 2-cup glass measure, combine 1 small can (8 oz.) **tomato**

(Continued on page 70)

MICROWAVE EGG BASICS

For successful eggs, keep in mind two important precautions: pay close attention to timing — mere seconds can make all the difference — and NEVER microwave an egg in its shell.

In the microwave, the yolk cooks faster than the white. The yolk, which has a higher fat content than the white, absorbs more microwave energy. This explains why it's important to stir scrambled eggs for even cooking and to puncture the fine membrane over the yolk of a poached or fried egg to prevent explosion.

Here we present basic methods for poaching, scrambling, and frying eggs to perfection in a microwave oven. We did all our testing with large eggs.

POACHED EGGS

Eggs poach to plump perfection with our method of microwaving each one in its own 10-ounce custard cup. Success depends mainly on two things: Be sure the water in the cups has reached a full boil, with bubbles breaking the surface, before you add the eggs. And never forget to prick the membrane that covers each yolk.

For 1 egg, pour ¼ cup hot tap water and ¼ teaspoon white vinegar into a 10-ounce custard cup. Microwave, uncovered, on **HIGH (100%)** for 1 minute or until boiling. Carefully crack 1 egg into boiling liquid. With a fork, prick egg yolk through membrane two times; then cover dish tightly with plastic wrap. Microwave on **HIGH (100%)** for 30 seconds. Remove from oven and let stand, covered, for 2 minutes. If you prefer your egg firmer, let stand for 3 to 4 more minutes. To serve, lift egg from water with a slotted spoon.

For 2 eggs, proceed as above, cooking each egg in its own custard cup; cooking time is the same.

For 3 or 4 eggs, measure water and vinegar into containers and arrange in a circle on a flat 12-inch plate — this makes it easy to remove the eggs from the oven quickly when they're cooked. It will take about 3½ to 4 minutes total for liquid in each cup to reach boiling. Proceed as above, adding 30 seconds cooking time for each additional egg (3 eggs, 1½ minutes; 4 eggs, 2 minutes).

FLUFFY SCRAMBLED EGGS

The eggs should be still moist when you remove them from the oven — they'll continue to cook briefly upon standing. If after standing they're more moist than you like, microwave them for 15 to 30 more seconds. We recommend scrambling no more than 8 eggs at a time in the microwave.

We put butter in the recipe for flavor only. If you prefer to omit it, do so — the eggs will cook quite successfully without butter.

For each egg, place butter or margarine in a dish of the correct size, as directed below — possible candidates include custard cups or small casseroles. Microwave, uncovered, on **HIGH (100%)** for 30 to 45 seconds or until butter has melted. Crack eggs directly into dish. Add milk and beat with a wire whip until well blended. Microwave as directed below, stirring after every minute (after 25 seconds if you're cooking just one egg) to bring cooked portion to center of dish. Allow eggs to stand for 1 to 2 minutes before serving. Season to taste with salt and pepper.

Container	Butter or Margarine	Eggs	Milk or Water	Cooking Time
6 oz.	1 tsp.	1	1 Tbsp.	45 secs.– 1 min.
10 oz.	2 tsp.	2	2 Tbsp.	1¼ mins.–1½ mins.
1 qt.	1 Tbsp.	4	3 Tbsp.	2½ mins.–3¼ mins.
1 qt.	1½ Tbsp.	6	¼ cup	3½ mins.–4¼ mins.
1½ qt.	2 Tbsp.	8	⅓ cup	4½ mins.–5¼ mins.

FRIED EGGS

Given the size of most microwave browning dishes, we recommend frying no more than two eggs at a time. Microwave a browning dish on **HIGH (100%)** for 2 minutes. Carefully remove dish (the bottom is very hot) to a heatproof surface. Over bottom of hot dish, evenly spread 2 teaspoons butter or margarine per egg. Carefully crack 1 or 2 eggs into dish. With a fork, prick egg yolks through membrane two times. Cover with a glass lid. Microwave on **HIGH (100%)** for 30 to 45 seconds per egg (if cooking 2 eggs, rotate dish ¼ turn after 30 seconds). Remove from oven and let stand, covered, for 2 to 3 minutes before serving. Season to taste.

sauce, and ¼ teaspoon each **garlic powder, ground cumin,** and **oregano leaves**; stir to blend. Microwave, uncovered, on **HIGH (100%)** for 2 minutes (stirring after 1 minute) or until heated through. Makes 1 cup.

MACARONI & CHEESE

With its gentle flavors and creamy texture, this macaroni and cheese dish may become one of your favorites. Serve this cheesy entrée with a crisp green salad, sliced tomatoes, and crusty bread.

- 3 **cups water**
- 1 **teaspoon butter or margarine**
- 2 **cups uncooked elbow macaroni**
- 3 **cups (12 oz.) shredded Cheddar cheese**
- 2 **teaspoons all-purpose flour**
- 1 **tablespoon butter or margarine**
- ½ **cup milk**
- 1 **teaspoon salt**
  Pepper

In a 3-quart casserole, combine water and the 1 teaspoon butter. Cover with a lid or plastic wrap. Microwave on **HIGH (100%)** for 5 to 6 minutes or until water boils. Stir in macaroni. Cover with a lid or pleated plastic wrap (page 7). Microwave on **HIGH (100%)** for 10 minutes, stirring after 5 minutes. Let stand, covered, for 5 minutes (macaroni should be **al dente**). If undercooked, microwave, on **HIGH (100%)** for 3 to 4 more minutes.

Toss cheese and flour together, then stir into macaroni along with the 1 tablespoon butter, milk, and salt. Season to taste with pepper. Cover with wax paper. Microwave on **HIGH (100%)** for 3 to 6 minutes (stirring after every 2 minutes) or until sauce thickens. Stir before serving. Makes 4 servings.

ITALIAN-STYLE FONDUE

(Pictured on opposite page)

Though classic cheese fondue can be tricky, this aromatic tomato and herb-laced version won't disappoint. Meatballs, Italian sausage slices, crisp vegetables, bread sticks, and cubes of French bread make a cheerful variety of dippers.

- 4 **cups (1 lb.) shredded Longhorn cheese**
- ½ **cup grated Parmesan cheese**
- 4 **teaspoons cornstarch**
- ¼ **cup butter or margarine**
- 1 **medium-size onion, finely chopped**
- 1 **clove garlic, minced or pressed**
- 1 **large can (16 oz.) stewed tomatoes**
- 1 **teaspoon dry basil**
- ½ **teaspoon oregano leaves**
- ⅛ **teaspoon pepper**

In a small bowl, stir together cheeses, cornstarch; set aside.

Place butter in a round 3-quart casserole or fondue dish. Microwave uncovered, on **HIGH (100%)** for 1 minute. Stir in onion and garlic. Microwave, covered with wax paper, on **HIGH (100%)** for 6 minutes, stirring after 3 minutes. Stir in tomatoes, basil, oregano, and pepper. Cover with wax paper. Microwave on **HIGH (100%)** for 2 minutes or until steaming.

Gradually add cheese mixture, stirring until cheese is completely melted. Microwave, covered, on **HIGH (100%)** for 2 minutes; beat vigorously with a wire whip. Microwave, uncovered, on **HIGH (100%)** for 4 minutes (beat after 2 minutes) or until fondue is thick and bubbly.

To reheat, microwave, covered, on **MEDIUM (50%)** for 1 minute (stirring after 30 seconds) or until heated through. Makes 4 servings.

HAM QUICHE

Light and tender quiche is one of those elusive delicacies that you can easily overcook in a microwave. But here's a recipe that's sure to reward you with delicious results. Follow it exactly, since we developed it specifically for the microwave.

- 2½ **cups (10 oz.) shredded Swiss cheese**
- 9-**inch baked pastry shell, 1½ inches deep, in glass, ceramic, or plastic dish**
- 1 **package (4 oz.) cooked ham, diced**
- 1 **cup half-and-half (light cream) or whipping cream**
- ½ **teaspoon salt**
- ⅛ **teaspoon white pepper**
- 3 **eggs**
- 2 **teaspoons freeze-dried chives**
- ⅛ **teaspoon ground nutmeg**

Sprinkle half the cheese over bottom of baked pastry shell; cover with ham, then with remaining cheese; set aside.

Pour half-and-half into a 2-cup glass measure. Add salt, pepper, and eggs; with a wire whip, beat until well blended. Microwave, uncovered, on **HIGH (100%)** for 2 minutes, stirring after 1 minute. Gradually pour hot egg mixture into pastry shell. Sprinkle with chives and nutmeg.

Microwave, uncovered, on **HIGH (100%)** for 7 to 9 minutes (rotating dish ¼ turn after every 4 minutes) or until center jiggles slightly when plate is gently shaken. (Upon standing, center will set.) Let stand, uncovered, for 10 minutes before serving. Makes 4 to 6 servings.

Sure to become a family favorite, Italian-style Fondue (recipe on this page) heats up in minutes — and you can reheat it in the microwave without worrying about the cheese separating. Tasty dippers include (clockwise from upper right) carrot sticks, green onion, zucchini rounds, celery sticks, mushrooms, Italian sausage chunks, bread sticks, and strips of bell pepper.

Sweets & Breakfast Treats

Cakes, coffee cakes, and muffins puff dramatically, custards and pie fillings thicken to perfection, liqueur-enhanced fruit desserts heat effortlessly — these are just a few of the sweet miracles your microwave can perform. In this chapter we also include some quick, simplified techniques for making an array of candies and fruit jams.

Before you begin, though, read through the tips below and let them guide you to good results with sweets and muffins.

TIPS AND TECHNIQUES

○ **Wax-paper-lined dishes.** If a cake is to be turned out of the dish before it has cooled completely, the bottom of the cake dish should be lined with wax paper.

To cut wax paper to size, set the dish on a piece of wax paper and trace around the outside of the dish; then cut the paper just inside the line. Dab a little shortening on the bottom of the dish and fit in the paper — the shortening prevents the paper from slipping when you pour in the batter.

○ **Shielding with foil.** Cakes baked in rectangular and square baking dishes can become overcooked and hard at the corners. Prevent this by shielding the corners with small foil triangles.

To make them, cut a piece of foil 5½ by 11 inches. Bring one corner of the foil up even with the top of the long edge, forming a triangle; fold over three more times. Cut foil along the folds into four triangles.

After pouring the batter into the dish, place a foil triangle on each corner, covering 1½ to 2 inches of the batter; tuck the remaining foil under the rim of the dish. The foil shields are removed in the final stage of baking according to each recipe.

○ **Disguising pale muffins, cakes, and bar cookies.** These cook so quickly there's no chance for browning. It's no problem with a batter that's naturally dark, like chocolate or spice, but you may want to disguise the pale appearance of other kinds by using a topping or frosting.

○ **Doneness test for muffins, cakes, and cookies.** Always check for doneness at the minimum time given in each recipe — overcooking toughens bakery products. Muffins, cakes, and bar cookies should spring back when lightly pressed in the center. If you see moist spots, touch one or two places — they should come off on your finger and the cake underneath should look dry. Moist spots will evaporate upon standing. (If the cake is still doughy underneath the spots, the product requires additional baking.)

It's helpful to use a glass baking dish for cakes and bar cookies because you can check the bottom for doneness; the center should show very little unbaked batter. If there seems to be a large uncooked area in the center, shield the corners and microwave on **HIGH (100%)** for one more minute.

○ **Doughy centers in cakes and bar cookies.** Some of the microwave ovens we used in testing our recipes left the center of cakes and bar cookies doughy. If you have this problem with your oven, place an inverted saucer or plate in the center of the microwave. Place the baking dish on the saucer and microwave according to the recipe.

○ **Standing time for muffins, cakes, and bar cookies.** These bakery products need standing time to finish cooking. Muffins won't have soggy bottoms if they're removed from their baking dish and placed on a metal rack immediately after baking. Let them stand for a few minutes to finish cooking.

Place cakes and bar cookies on a heatproof surface for standing time. It's important to cover them with wax paper while they're standing; this retains moisture and distributes the heat more evenly to finish the cooking process.

○ **Reheating bread products.** The microwave reheats baked breads, sweet rolls, and doughnuts easily and quickly — so quickly, in fact, that you'll need to be very vigilant. It takes just 10 to 15 seconds on **HIGH** to reheat *each* roll or bread-slice.

To reheat a roll, wrap it in a paper towel or paper napkin (to prevent soggy bottom) and heat only until the outside surface feels warm to the touch. If heated too long, it becomes tough and hard when cool.

For several rolls, line a wicker basket (no metal staples) with a paper towel or a cloth napkin. Place the rolls (we recommend no more than eight at a time) in the basket and cover them with another towel or napkin. Microwave on **HIGH (100%)** for 10 to 15 seconds a roll.

Remember that the sugar in fillings and icings attracts more microwaves than the pastry or bread surrounding them; so to avoid burning yourself, allow a few minutes standing time.

○ **Cooking custard-type desserts.** Creamy and delicate, these desserts can be baked without the usual water bath; for even cooking, you'll need to stir them or rotate the dish.

○ **Doneness test for custard-type desserts.** They should jiggle slightly in the center when the plate is gently shaken — they will set upon standing. Cool these desserts for a few minutes, then cover them loosely and refrigerate.

○ **Microwaving fruit desserts.** Nutritious fruit desserts microwave beautifully and make a delightful finale for almost any

meal. Remove these desserts from the microwave while the fruit is still slightly firm, because they'll continue to cook upon standing.

○ **Not recommended for microwaving.**

Breads: Simply put, the quality and texture of conventionally baked breads are far superior to those of microwaved breads. Microwaved breads have all the characteristics you don't want in breads — they may be temperamental, tough, and chewy, and taste as if they'd been steamed.

Pastry shells: We don't recommend baking pastry shells in the microwave, since the results are often tough and brittle. Instead, use a conventional oven. But do use your microwave for the pie filling while you're baking the pastry shell conventionally. Then combine the two, as we've done with our Sugarless Apple Pie (page 86) and Spicy Pumpkin Pie (page 86).

Popovers, cream puffs, and angel food cakes: These and other products that depend on eggs for leavening should be baked in a conventional oven.

BLUEBERRY-ORANGE MUFFINS

Wide-awake fruit flavors make these muffins the perfect companions for a hearty breakfast or brunch. Since our recipe calls for canned blueberries, you can serve these lightly sweetened little breads the year around.

(Continued on page 75)

Nut topping (recipe follows)
2 cups all-purpose flour
¼ cup sugar
2 teaspoons baking powder
¼ teaspoon baking soda
½ teaspoon salt
¾ cup orange juice
¼ cup salad oil
1 egg
1 teaspoon grated orange peel
1 can (15 oz.) blueberries, drained well

Prepare nut topping; set aside.

In a large bowl, stir together flour, sugar, baking powder, baking soda, and salt; make a well in center and set aside.

In another bowl, combine orange juice and oil. Add egg and orange peel and beat lightly. Pour into well in flour mixture and stir just to moisten (mixture should be lumpy). Gently stir in blueberries.

Spoon half the batter into a paper-cup-lined microwave cupcaker or six paper-lined 6-ounce custard cups, filling each cup ⅔ full. Sprinkle evenly with nut topping. Arrange custard cups in a circle on a large, flat plate.

Microwave, uncovered, on **HIGH (100%)** for 3 to 4 minutes. If muffins are baking unevenly, rotate dish ¼ turn after 2 minutes. Check for doneness at minimum time — muffins should spring back when pressed in center; moist spots will disappear upon standing.

Immediately remove muffins from cups and let stand on a wire rack for 2 minutes before serving. Repeat with remaining batter. Makes 12 to 14 muffins.

Nutty topping. In a small bowl, stir together ¼ cup firmly packed **brown sugar**, ⅓ cup chopped **nuts**, and ½ teaspoon **ground cinnamon**.

Capture the essence of fresh fruit in easy Microwave Jam (pages 76 and 77) and grace your table with their sweetness the year around. Choose from 11 variations — here we feature (starting from top) Apricot, Strawberry, Purple Plum & Orange, and Berry.

READY-BAKE BRAN MUFFINS

For busy cooks we offer these wholesome, fruit-laced muffins that can be table-ready in only a few minutes. The secret is a make-ahead batter that you store in the refrigerator for up to two weeks, using only as much as needed each time.

3 cups whole bran cereal
1 cup boiling water
2 eggs, lightly beaten
2 cups buttermilk
½ cup salad oil
1 cup raisins, currants, chopped pitted dates, or chopped pitted prunes
2 teaspoons baking soda
½ teaspoon salt
1 cup sugar
2½ cups all-purpose flour

In a large bowl, combine cereal with boiling water and stir thoroughly. Let cool, then stir in eggs, buttermilk, oil, and fruit; blend well.

In another large bowl, mix together baking soda, salt, sugar, and flour; then stir in bran mixture. Cover tightly and refrigerate for up to 2 weeks; before using, stir batter to distribute fruit evenly.

To bake, spoon refrigerated batter into a paper-cup-lined microwave cupcaker or paper-lined 6-ounce custard cups, filling each cup half full. If using custard cups, arrange them in a circle on a large, flat plate.

Prepare desired number of cups and microwave on **HIGH (100%)** for time indicated on chart (next column). If muffins are baking unevenly, rotate dish ¼ turn after 2 minutes. Check for doneness at minimum time — muffins should spring back when lightly pressed in center; moist spots will disappear upon standing.

Immediately remove muffins

from cups and let stand on a wire rack for 2 minutes before serving. Makes about 3 dozen muffins.

Muffins	Time
1	45 seconds to 1 minute
2	1 to 1½ minutes
3	1½ to 2 minutes
4	2 to 2½ minutes
5	2½ to 3 minutes
6	3 to 4 minutes
7	4 to 5 minutes

SOUR CREAM COFFEE CAKE

(Pictured on page 66)

Light and fluffy, buttery and rich, this is one coffee cake that won't last long. The batter will cook to the top of the baking dish — it won't spill over.

½ cup *each* firmly packed brown sugar and chopped walnuts
¾ teaspoon ground cinnamon
¾ cup butter or margarine, softened
¾ cup granulated sugar
3 eggs
¾ cup sour cream
1 teaspoon vanilla
1½ cups all-purpose flour
½ teaspoon *each* baking powder and baking soda
¼ teaspoon salt

Lightly grease the bottom of an 8 by 2½-inch round baking dish or a 2-quart casserole dish. Grease the outside of an 8-ounce glass and place in center of dish; set aside.

In a small bowl, combine brown sugar, walnuts, and cinnamon. Sprinkle half the nut mixture over bottom of baking dish.

In a medium-size bowl, beat butter and granulated sugar with an electric mixer on medium speed until fluffy. Add eggs, one at a time, and beat well. Beat in sour cream and vanilla; then add flour, baking

(Continued on page 78)

FRESH FRUIT JAMS

(Pictured on page 74)

With their jewel-bright colors and rich fruit flavors, homemade jams are understandably a family favorite. And with a microwave, jam preparation goes so quickly that you can boil up a batch just before breakfast.

Unlike jams conventionally cooked, microwave jams don't scorch, nor do they require constant stirring — they do need some attention though, so you'll want to stay in the kitchen.

Since microwaves are particularly attracted to sugar molecules, there is danger of boil-over unless you use a generously oversized container. Our favorite is a 2-quart (8-cup) glass measure. Since it requires no pot holders, the bowl is easy to remove from the oven; its handle and spout simplify transferring the hot, bubbly jam into hot sterilized jars.

An alternative is to use a 2½ or 3-quart ceramic or glass casserole or soufflé dish — but these will get hot, so keep thick pot holders handy.

With its variations, this recipe makes 12 different fresh fruit jams. For the most flavorful results, choose ripe fruits at the peak of their maturity; less-ripe fruits won't impart enough sweetness to the jam.

Most of the fruits used in jam need to be chopped (some, such as berries, are crushed instead). You may want to experiment with chopping fruit in a food processor, but even cooking depends on the fruit's being uniformly chopped, and we found that chopping by hand produced the greatest uniformity.

Refrigerated, these jams will keep well for several months; freeze them for longer storage. Though it takes far more time and effort, you can also put up these jams in traditional canning jars for lengthy shelf storage.

However you plan to store the jam, you'll need to sterilize the jars. Do this on the range — the microwave can't provide the constant high heat necessary for this, nor can it melt the paraffin used for sealing some kinds of jars.

Don't attempt to double the recipe or alter the 2-cup quantity in any way — the relationships of quantity, timing, and container are crucial and have been worked out with precision. If you have an abundant harvest, you can prepare fruit and mix it with sugar and flavoring according to the recipes that follow, and then freeze it. Later, thaw a portion and complete the recipe for fresh fruit jam at any time of year.

MICROWAVE JAM

Diced or crushed fruit and flavorings (recipes follow)
1½ cups sugar
½ teaspoon butter or margarine

Prepare fruit and flavorings and place in a 2-quart glass measure or 2½ to 3-quart casserole. Add sugar and butter; stir thoroughly.

Cover with wax paper. Microwave on **HIGH (100%)** for about 6 minutes or until mixture comes to a boil. Remove wax paper and stir fruit mixture. Microwave, uncovered, on **HIGH (100%)** for time indicated on chart below.

Jam will set to good consistency if it begins to coat a metal spoon. Test by dripping fruit mixture from side of spoon; droplets should be thick.

Or put 1 tablespoon of the mixture in a custard cup after minimum time; place in freezer for 5 to 7 minutes or in refrigerator for 15 minutes; test consistency. If it's not thick enough, reheat to boiling, then microwave, uncovered, on **HIGH (100%)** for 2 more minutes; test consistency again.

Pour into hot sterilized jars, filling each ⅔ full. Cool, cover with a lid, and refrigerate or freeze. Makes about 2 cups.

FRUIT	TIME
Apple	5– 7 minutes
Apricot	10–12 minutes
Apricot & pineapple	13–15 minutes
Berry	13–15 minutes
Blueberry	9–11 minutes
Cherry	9–11 minutes
Spiced fig & orange	13–15 minutes
Peach or nectarine	13–15 minutes
Peach & plum	13–15 minutes
Plum	9–11 minutes
Purple plum & orange	9–11 minutes
Strawberry	15–20 minutes

Apple jam.   Peel and core about **4 apples** (Gravenstein, Jonathan, McIntosh, or Newtown Pippin). Dice to make 2 cups. Add 1 tablespoon **lemon juice** and 1 teaspoon **ground cinnamon**.

Apricot jam.   Remove pits from about 1 pound **apricots**; chop to make 2 cups. Add 2 table-spoons **lemon juice**.

Apricot & pineapple jam.   Remove pits from about ¾ pound **apricots**; chop to make 1½ cups. Combine with ½ cup canned **unsweetened crushed pineapple**. Add 1 tablespoon **lemon juice**.

Berry jam.   Crush about 3 cups **raspberries**, blackberries, boysenberries, or olallieberries; or use a combination of half raspberries and half of any of the black berries. You should have 2 cups. Add 1 tablespoon **lemon juice**.

Blueberry jam.   Slightly crush about 3 cups **blueberries**, to make 2 cups. Add ¼ cup **lemon juice**, ½ teaspoon grated **lemon peel**, ¼ teaspoon **ground cinnamon**.

Cherry (sweet varieties) jam.   Pit about 1 pound **cherries** and cut into halves to make 2 cups. Add ¼ cup **lemon juice**, ½ teaspoon grated **lemon peel**, and a 2-inch **cinnamon stick** (or ½ teaspoon ground cinnamon). Remove cinnamon stick after cooking.

Spiced fig & orange jam.   Dice 8 to 10 **figs** to make 1½ cups; combine with ½ cup peeled, seeded, and chopped **orange** to make 2 cups *total*. Add 1½ teaspoons grated **orange peel**, 3 tablespoons **lemon juice**, and ¼ teaspoon *each* ground **ginger**, **cloves**, and **cinnamon**.

Peach or nectarine jam.   Remove pits from about 1 pound **peaches** or nectarines; chop to make 2 cups. Add 1 tablespoon **lemon juice**. If desired, stir in 2 drops **almond extract** after cooking.

Peach & plum jam.   Remove pits from about ½ pound *each* **peaches** and **plums**; chop to make ¾ cup of each fruit; combine with ½ cup seeded and finely chopped **orange**, including peel.

Plum jam.   Remove pits from about 1 pound **plums**; chop to make 2 cups. Add 1 tablespoon **lemon juice**.

Purple plum & orange jam.   Remove pits from about 1 pound **purple prune plums**; chop to make 1½ cups; combine with ½ cup peeled, seeded, and finely chopped **orange**. Add 2 teaspoons grated **orange peel**, 1 tablespoon **lemon juice**, and ⅛ teaspoon **ground cinnamon**. (For a bittersweet flavor, substitute ½ cup unpeeled, finely chopped **orange** for the peeled orange and omit grated peel.)

Strawberry jam.   Hull about 3½ cups whole **strawberries** and crush to make 2 cups. Add 1½ tablespoons **lemon juice**.

powder, baking soda, and salt. Beat until well blended.

Spoon half the batter into prepared baking dish and spread it evenly over nut mixture. Sprinkle remaining nut mixture over batter, then spoon remaining batter over nut mixture and spread evenly.

Microwave, uncovered, on **MEDIUM-HIGH (70%)** for 9 to 12 minutes or until top looks dry and cake pulls away from side of dish. Let stand for 5 minutes. Remove glass from center and invert cake onto a serving plate. Cover cake loosely with plastic wrap. Let stand for 30 minutes before serving. Makes 10 to 12 servings.

BLUEBERRY COFFEE CAKE

Lightly sweetened, studded with blueberries, and laced with cinnamon, this moist cake will wake up the sleepiest appetite and make breakfast a very special occasion.

Cinnamon sugar
(recipe follows)
6 tablespoons butter or margarine, softened
½ cup sugar
1 egg
½ teaspoon vanilla
1 cup all-purpose flour
2 teaspoons baking powder
½ teaspoon salt
1 teaspoon ground cinnamon
¼ cup milk
1 can (15 oz.) blueberries, drained well

Prepare cinnamon sugar; set aside.

In a medium-size bowl, beat butter and sugar until fluffy; add egg and vanilla and beat well. Stir in flour, baking powder, salt, cinnamon, and milk. Gently stir in blueberries. Spread batter evenly in a lightly

greased 9-inch square baking dish. Sprinkle with cinnamon sugar. Shield each corner with a 2-inch triangle of foil (page 72).

Microwave on **MEDIUM (50%)** for 6 minutes, rotating dish ¼ turn after 3 minutes. Microwave on **HIGH (100%)** for 2 to 4 minutes, removing foil shields after 2 minutes. Cake should spring back when lightly pressed in center; moist spots, when touched, should come off on your finger and cake underneath should be dry.

Cover with wax paper and let stand for 15 minutes; cut into squares. Makes 9 servings.

Cinnamon sugar. In a small bowl, mix together 2 tablespoons **sugar** and 1 teaspoon **ground cinnamon.**

ALMOND FUDGE TORTE

(Pictured on opposite page)

Sinfully rich, this easy chocolate torte has pastry-shop looks and a brownielike texture. The almond paste, available in some supermarkets or in specialty food stores, makes the torte especially moist and chewy.

2 tablespoons water
1 teaspoon instant coffee powder
1 box (8 oz.) semisweet baking chocolate
3 eggs
¾ cup sugar
½ cup (¼ lb.) butter or margarine, softened
⅓ cup (about 2 oz.) almond paste
½ cup all-purpose flour
1 tablespoon butter or margarine
Sliced almonds (optional)

Cut a circle of wax paper to fit the bottom of an 8-inch round baking dish; set aside.

In a 10-ounce custard cup, place water, coffee powder, and half the chocolate. Cover with wax paper. Microwave on **HIGH (100%)** for 1¼ minutes or until chocolate melts; stir to blend, then set aside.

Separate eggs, placing whites in a medium-size bowl and yolks in a small cup. Beat egg whites just until soft, moist peaks form. In another bowl, beat butter and sugar until fluffy. Crumble almond paste over butter mixture. Beat until mixture is almost smooth (there will still be some lumps of paste); then beat in egg yolks. Stir in chocolate mixture and flour. Fold in beaten whites, a third at a time, just until blended. Spoon mixture into prepared baking dish; smooth top.

Microwave, uncovered, on **MEDIUM (50%)** for 13 to 15 minutes or until a wooden pick inserted in center comes out clean. Top will look moist, but should spring back when gently touched. Let cool in dish on a wire rack for 15 minutes, then invert onto a serving plate to cool completely.

Meanwhile, place remaining chocolate and the 1 tablespoon butter in a 10-ounce custard cup. Cover with wax paper. Microwave on **HIGH (100%)** for 1½ minutes; stir to blend. If it does not blend easily, microwave on **HIGH (100%)** for 30 more seconds. Let cool for 30 minutes, then spread over top and sides of cake. Garnish with nuts, if desired.

Let stand until chocolate hardens (2 to 4 hours at room temperature; 30 to 45 minutes, if refrigerated). Serve at room temperature. Makes 10 servings.

Choose — if you can — from a trio of sweet treats for afternoon tea, a company dinner finale, or dessert any time of day. Or offer all three — cream cheese-frosted Carrot Cake (recipe on page 80), Almond Fudge Torte (recipe on this page), and Cheesecake Tarts (recipe on page 88).

CARROT CAKE

(Pictured on page 79)

The sweet flavor of shredded carrots abounds in this rich-tasting and nutritious treat. Crown it with a cream cheese frosting laced with orange peel. For a festive occasion or just family fare, this moist carrot cake is sure to be a favorite.

1½ cups sugar
1 cup salad oil
4 eggs
1 teaspoon vanilla
1½ cups all-purpose flour
2½ teaspoons ground cinnamon
¼ teaspoon ground nutmeg
2 teaspoons baking powder
1½ teaspoons baking soda
1 teaspoon salt
2 cups shredded carrots, lightly packed
   Cream cheese frosting (recipe follows)

In a medium-size bowl, stir together sugar and oil; beat in eggs, one at a time, then stir in vanilla. Stir in flour, cinnamon, nutmeg, baking powder, baking soda, salt, and carrots. Pour batter into a lightly greased 10-inch non-metallic bundt dish.

Microwave, uncovered, on **MEDIUM (50%)** for 12 minutes, rotating dish ¼ turn every 4 minutes. Microwave on **HIGH (100%)** for 2 to 4 minutes. Cake should spring back when lightly pressed; moist spots, when touched, should come off on your finger and cake underneath should be dry. Cake should also pull away from side of dish.

Let stand for 15 minutes on a wire rack, then invert onto a serving platter. Cover loosely with wax paper. Let cool completely.

Prepare cream cheese frosting and spread over top of cooled cake. Refrigerate until needed. Makes about 12 servings.

Cream cheese frosting. In a medium-size bowl, place 2 small packages (3 oz. *each*) **cream cheese** (softened), 6 tablespoons **butter** or margarine (softened), 1 tablespoon grated **orange peel**, and 1 teaspoon **vanilla**; blend well. Stir in 2 cups sifted **powdered sugar** until well blended. (Or put all ingredients into a food processor and whirl until well blended.)

CHOCOLATE APPLESAUCE CAKE

Spicy, moist, and tender, this cake travels well. It adds a delicious touch of glory to a brown bag lunch — and you'll hear rave reviews at day's end.

½ cup salad oil
2 squares (1 oz. *each*) semi-sweet baking chocolate
2 cups all-purpose flour
1 cup granulated sugar
1½ tablespoons cornstarch
2 teaspoons baking soda
1 teaspoon ground cinnamon
½ teaspoon ground nutmeg
¼ teaspoon *each* salt and ground cloves
½ cup raisins
1 cup chopped nuts
1 can (16 oz.) applesauce
1 egg, lightly beaten
   Powdered sugar (optional)

In a 10-ounce custard cup, place oil and chocolate. Cover with wax paper. Microwave on **HIGH (100%)** for 1½ minutes. Stir mixture until chocolate melts; set aside.

In a medium-size bowl, stir together flour, sugar, cornstarch, baking soda, cinnamon, nutmeg, salt, cloves, raisins, and nuts. Add applesauce, chocolate mixture, and egg; blend well. Pour into a lightly greased 7 by 11-inch baking dish. Shield each corner with a 2-inch triangle of foil (page 72).

Microwave on **MEDIUM (50%)** for 8 minutes, rotating dish ½ turn after 4 minutes. Microwave on **HIGH (100%)** for 2 to 4 minutes, removing foil shields after 2 minutes. Cake should spring back when lightly pressed in center; moist spots, when touched, should come off on your finger and cake underneath should be dry.

Let cool in dish. Before serving, sprinkle with powdered sugar, if desired. Makes 6 to 8 servings.

SPICY STEAMED PUDDING

(Pictured on front cover)

Traditionally served as the sweet finale to a Christmas dinner, this old-fashioned steamed pudding can brighten other special occasions as well. Our version, moistened with applesauce or persimmon purée, steam-cooks in the microwave in a third of the conventional cooking time — and without a water bath.

Top small wedges of pudding with the accompanying tart lemon sauce, or simply dust with powdered sugar.

Lemon sauce (recipe follows)
- ½ cup (¼ lb.) butter or margarine, softened
- 1 cup sugar
- 2 eggs
- 1 cup applesauce or persimmon purée (whirl about 3 seeded and peeled ripe persimmons in a blender until smooth)
- 1 teaspoon *each* vanilla and lemon juice
- 2 tablespoons water
- 1 cup all-purpose flour
- 1 teaspoon ground cinnamon
- 2 teaspoons baking soda
- ¼ teaspoon *each* salt and ground allspice
- ½ cup chopped nuts
- 1 cup raisins or chopped pitted dates

Powdered sugar (optional)

Prepare lemon sauce; cover and refrigerate until needed.

Generously grease a 6-cup ring mold. (Or grease the outside of a 6-ounce glass and place in the center of a 1½-quart casserole greased on the bottom.) Set aside.

In a medium-size bowl, beat butter and sugar until fluffy. Beat in eggs; then mix in applesauce, vanilla, lemon juice, and water. Add flour, cinnamon, baking soda, salt, and allspice; blend well. Stir in nuts and raisins. Pour batter into prepared mold and cover tightly with plastic wrap.

Microwave on **MEDIUM-HIGH (70%)** for 23 minutes, rotating dish ½ turn after 11 minutes. Or microwave on **MEDIUM (50%)** for 20 minutes, rotating dish ½ turn after 10 minutes, then microwave on **HIGH (100%)** for 3 minutes.

Let stand, covered, for 15 minutes. To serve, invert hot pudding onto a plate; serve with lemon sauce or dust with powdered sugar. If made ahead, store at room temperature for up to 2 days. To re-steam, cover with plastic wrap and microwave on **MEDIUM**

(50%) for 15 minutes. Makes 8 to 10 servings.

Lemon sauce. Place ½ cup **butter** or margarine in a 4-cup measuring cup. Microwave, uncovered, on **HIGH (100%)** for 1 minute. With a wire whip, beat in 1 cup **sugar**, ¼ cup **lemon juice**, 1 teaspoon grated **lemon peel**, 1 tablespoon **water**, and 1 **egg**; blend well. Microwave, uncovered, on **HIGH (100%)** for 4 to 5 minutes, beating with wire whip every minute. (Upon cooling, sauce will thicken.) Makes 1½ cups.

CHOCOLATE BROWNIES

These popular bar cookies take only 15 minutes from ingredients stage to fresh-baked results when cooked in the microwave. The batter may rise unevenly, looking lopsided at first, but without any rotating, it evens out to a smooth layer by the end of the baking time.

For a snack, serve these delicious, nut-studded morsels plain; for dessert, you can top generous squares with scoops of ice cream.

- 2 squares (1 oz. *each*) unsweetened baking chocolate
- ½ cup butter or margarine
- 2 eggs
- 1 cup sugar
- ½ teaspoon vanilla
- ½ cup plus 2 tablespoons all-purpose flour
- ⅛ teaspoon salt
- ½ cup chopped nuts

In a 10-ounce custard cup, place chocolate and butter. Cover with wax paper. Microwave on **HIGH (100%)** for 1¼ to 1½ minutes or until butter melts. Stir mixture until chocolate melts; set aside.

In a medium-size bowl, beat

eggs with an electric mixer until slightly thickened. Gradually add sugar and vanilla; beat until thickened. Beat in chocolate mixture, flour, and salt. Stir in nuts. Pour batter into a lightly greased 8-inch square baking dish.

Microwave, uncovered, on **MEDIUM-HIGH (70%)** for 8 to 10 minutes. Brownies should spring back when lightly pressed in center; moist spots, when touched, should come off on your finger and cake underneath should be dry. Cover with wax paper and let cool completely before cutting. Makes 16 bars.

DRIED FRUIT & NUT BARS

Laden with nuts and dried fruits, these nourishing dessert bars make a wonderful brown bag treat. Cut bars while they're still warm, but allow to cool completely before dusting them with powdered sugar.

- 2 eggs
- ½ cup firmly packed brown sugar
- ½ teaspoon vanilla
- 3 tablespoons butter or margarine, melted
- ½ cup all-purpose flour
- ½ teaspoon *each* baking powder, salt, and grated orange peel
- 1 cup finely chopped walnuts
- 2 cups finely chopped pitted dates (or 1 cup finely chopped pitted dates and ½ cup *each* finely chopped dried apricots and raisins)

Powdered sugar

(Continued on page 83)

In a medium-sized bowl, beat eggs until foamy; then beat in sugar, vanilla, and butter. Stir in flour, baking powder, salt, and orange peel; then mix in nuts and fruit. Spread batter evenly in a 9-inch square baking dish. Shield each corner with a 2-inch triangle of foil (page 72).

Microwave on **MEDIUM (50%)** for 6 minutes, rotating dish ¼ turn after 3 minutes. Microwave on **HIGH (100%)** for 4 to 6 minutes, removing foil shields after 2 minutes. Cookies should spring back when lightly pressed in center; moist spots, when touched, should come off on your finger and cookies underneath should be dry.

Cover with wax paper and let stand for 15 minutes. Cut into 1 by 2-inch bars while still warm. Let cool in dish, then dust each bar with powdered sugar. Makes about 32 bars.

NUTTY CHOCOLATE CHIP BARS

We've transformed everybody's favorite cookie into something even better — rich, crunchy, cakelike bars liberally laced and frosted with melted chocolate morsels. Kids will love them with a cold glass of milk after school. They'll disappear fast, so keep extra ingredients on hand.

Irresistible confections tempt you to nibble as you pack them up for holiday gifts. They include (clockwise from upper left) Peanut Brittle, Quick Chocolate Fudge, Almond Toffee, Chocolate Truffles, and Candied Walnuts. The recipes are on pages 84 and 85.

½ cup butter or margarine, softened
¾ cup firmly packed brown sugar
2 eggs
1 teaspoon vanilla
1 cup all-purpose flour
½ teaspoon *each* baking powder and salt
½ cup chopped walnuts
1 package (6 oz.) semisweet chocolate chips

In a medium-size bowl, beat butter and sugar until fluffy; beat in eggs and vanilla. Stir in flour, baking powder, and salt, then add nuts and the chocolate chips. Spread batter evenly in a lightly greased 9-inch square baking dish. Shield each corner with a 2-inch triangle of foil (page 72).

Microwave on **MEDIUM (50%)** for 4 minutes. Remove shields and microwave on **HIGH (100%)** for 1 to 2 minutes. Cookies should spring back when lightly pressed in center; moist spots, when touched, should come off on your finger and cookies underneath should be dry.

Place dish on a wire rack, cover with wax paper, and let cool completely; then cut into bars. Makes about 25 bars.

ZABAGLIONE CREAM

Velvety smooth and richly flavored with eggs and sherry, this Italian dessert custard is spooned into parfait glasses over whipped cream. The hot zabaglione and cold whipped cream make a winning combination.

⅔ cup whipping cream
5½ tablespoons sugar
½ cup dry sherry
8 egg yolks

In a medium-size bowl, combine cream with 1½ tablespoons of the sugar and whip until soft peaks form. Spoon cream evenly into 6 parfait glasses; set aside.

Pour sherry into a small measuring cup. Microwave, uncovered, on **HIGH (100%)** for 1 minute.

Place egg yolks in a medium-size bowl. Sprinkle with remaining 4 tablespoons sugar and beat until sugar dissolves. Gradually add hot sherry, beating constantly. Microwave, uncovered, on **MEDIUM (50%)** for 2 to 3 minutes (beating with a wire whip after every minute) or until thickened and smooth. Spoon custard evenly over whipped cream. Serve immediately. Makes 6 servings.

INDIVIDUAL BAKED CUSTARD

A favorite with children as well as with grownups, egg custard is an elegant dessert that bakes quickly in a microwave — without the bother of the usual hot water bath.

1⅓ cup milk
4 eggs
4 tablespoons sugar
1 teaspoon vanilla
Dash of salt
½ teaspoon ground nutmeg

Pour milk into a 4-cup glass measure or bowl. Add eggs, sugar, vanilla, and salt; beat with a wire whip until well blended. Microwave, uncovered, on **HIGH (100%)** for 2 minutes, stirring after 1 minute.

Meanwhile, place four 6-ounce custard cups or ramekins in a circle on a large, flat plate. Pour hot egg mixture into cups. Sprinkle with nutmeg. Microwave, uncovered, on **ME-**

(Continued on page 86)

THE CANDY BOX

(Pictured on page 82)

In just minutes, you can make irresistible candies in your microwave oven — for sweet-tooth indulgence at home or for holiday gift giving.

The only equipment you'll need is a wire whip or wooden spoon, a 2-quart glass measure (and pot holders, if you're using a 2-quart casserole). The capacity of the bowl should be at least three times the volume of the ingredients, since the syrup mixture gets extremely hot and bubbles up very high. You may want to use a candy thermometer for Peanut Brittle or Candied Walnuts (recipes below), but be sure **not** to put it in the microwave.

ALMOND TOFFEE

Irresistible to candy-lovers who like crunch in every bite, this butter-rich toffee is frosted with chocolate, then crowned with a sprinkling of finely chopped almonds. Don't substitute margarine — butter is essential to the flavor.

Butter
- ¾ cup butter
- 1 cup firmly packed brown sugar
- ¾ cup finely chopped almonds
- ½ cup semisweet chocolate chips

Line an 8-inch square baking dish with foil, extending it up and over two sides; butter foil lightly and set aside.

In a 2-quart glass measure, place butter and sugar. Microwave, uncovered, on **HIGH (100%)** for 1 minute. Beat with a wire whip until smooth; microwave, uncovered, on **HIGH (100%)** for 4 more minutes. Stir in ½ cup of the almonds. Microwave, uncovered, on **HIGH (100%)** for 2 minutes or until mixture thickens. (Watch carefully because sugar burns quickly.)

Stir with a wire whip. Place prepared dish on a flat surface and immediately pour in mixture. Sprinkle with chocolate chips and cover with plastic wrap for 4 minutes until chocolate melts.

Spread melted chocolate evenly over top and sprinkle with remaining ¼ cup almonds. Refrigerate, uncovered, until chocolate hardens. Remove toffee from dish and peel off foil. Break toffee into pieces, pack in shallow containers, cover, and refrigerate. Toffee will keep for several months in the refrigerator. Makes about 1 pound.

PEANUT BRITTLE

Crunchy golden brittle chock-full of whole peanuts is sure to be a family favorite. A 2-quart glass measure is the ideal cooking container for this candy — its handle allows you to pour out the hot syrup with one hand and spread it quickly with the other before the candy hardens.

- 1½ cups sugar
- ¾ cup light corn syrup
- ¼ teaspoon salt
- 1 tablespoon butter or margarine
- 2 cups dry roasted peanuts
- 1 teaspoon vanilla
- 1 teaspoon baking soda

Lightly grease a rimmed baking sheet and set aside.

In a 2-quart glass measure, stir together sugar and corn syrup until blended. Microwave, uncovered, on **HIGH (100%)** for 7 minutes, stirring after 3 minutes. Stir in salt, butter, peanuts, and vanilla. Microwave, uncovered, on **HIGH (100%)** for 5 to 6 minutes or until candy forms hard threads when dropped into a cup of cold water (or reaches hard crack stage — 300° on a candy thermometer).

Beat in baking soda (mixture will be bubbly and turn light tan). Immediately pour mixture onto prepared baking sheet and with a spatula, quickly spread out as thinly as possible.

For even thinner brittle, let mixture cool on baking sheet for 5 to 10 minutes (candy should be pliable). Lift candy slightly off baking sheet and stretch to desired thinness. Let cool for at least 1 hour. Break into pieces and store in an airtight container. Makes about 1½ pounds.

CANDIED WALNUTS

These spicy, sugared walnuts are a perfect dinner finale with a cup of espresso.

- 1 cup firmly packed brown sugar
- 2 tablespoons light corn syrup
- ¼ cup whipping cream
- ½ cup granulated sugar
- ¼ teaspoon salt
- ½ teaspoon ground allspice
- 2 tablepoons butter or margarine
- 2 teaspoons vanilla
- 3 cups walnut halves or quarters

Cover a baking sheet with foil; lightly grease foil and set aside.

In a 2-quart glass measure, combine brown sugar, corn syrup, cream, granulated sugar, salt, and allspice. Microwave, covered with wax paper, on **HIGH (100%)** for 4 to 6 minutes (stirring after 2 minutes) or until mixture reaches 240° on a candy thermometer.

With a wire whip, beat in butter and vanilla until smooth, then stir in walnut halves. Microwave, uncovered, on **HIGH (100%)** for 2 minutes. Pour candied walnuts onto prepared baking sheet; with a spatula, spread out in a single layer. Let cool until firm; then separate into individual pieces. Makes 3 cups.

QUICK CHOCOLATE FUDGE

Smooth, creamy, and scrumptious, this microwave fudge evokes the melt-in-your-mouth goodness of fudge from grandmother's kitchen.

- 1 box (1 lb.) powdered sugar
- ½ cup unsweetened cocoa
- ½ cup (¼ lb.) firm butter or margarine
- ¼ cup half-and-half (light cream)
- 2 teaspoons vanilla
- ¾ cup coarsely chopped nuts

Lightly grease an 8-inch square baking dish and set aside.

In a 1-quart glass bowl, combine sugar and cocoa. Cut butter into small pieces and dot over sugar mixture. Stir in half-and-half and vanilla. Cover with wax paper. Microwave on **HIGH (100%)** for 2 minutes. With a wooden spoon, stir hot mixture until butter melts, then beat vigorously with a spoon for 1 minute or until fudge loses some of its gloss.

Stir in ½ cup of the nuts. Pour fudge into prepared dish and spread it evenly. Sprinkle with remaining ¼ cup nuts, lightly pressing them into fudge. Refrigerate, uncovered, for 1 to 2 hours or until firm. Cut into squares. Place in tins, cover, and refrigerate. Makes about 1 pound.

CHOCOLATE TRUFFLES

Though related in name only to the little nuggets of sublime flavor that are unearthed under French oak trees, chocolate truffles rolled in cocoa look something like the French truffles and offer an equally exotic mouthful.

Prepare chocolate truffles a day in advance to give their flavors time to blend.

- 1 box (8 oz.) semisweet baking chocolate
- ½ cup whipping cream
- 2 tablespoons firm butter cut into 4 pieces
- 1 cup sifted powdered sugar
- 3 egg yolks
- 1½ teaspoons imitation rum or brandy extract
  Unsweetened cocoa, chopped nuts, shredded coconut, or chocolate sprinkles

In a 1-quart glass bowl, place chocolate, cream, and butter pieces. Cover with wax paper. Microwave on **HIGH (100%)** for 2 minutes; then beat with a wire whip until well blended.

Beat in sugar and egg yolks until mixture is smooth. Microwave, covered, on **MEDIUM (50%)** for 3 minutes (stirring every minute) or until slightly thickened. Beat in rum extract. Pour mixture into a 7 by 11-inch baking dish. Refrigerate for 2 hours. Candy mixture should roll easily between two fingers without sticking; if it feels sticky, refrigerate for 30 more minutes.

To make truffles, roll candy mixture, a teaspoon at a time, into balls; then roll in cocoa, nuts, coconut, or chocolate sprinkles. Place each truffle on a wax-paper-lined baking sheet or in individual paper candy cups and refrigerate for 1 hour or until hardened. Place in tins, cover, and refrigerate for up to 10 days or freeze for up to a month. Makes about 4 dozen.

DIUM (50%) for 6 to 9 minutes, rotating each cup ½ turn after 4 minutes. Custard should jiggle slightly in center when cup is gently shaken. (Upon standing, center will set.)

Cover with wax paper and let stand for 20 minutes, then serve. Or refrigerate, covered, until needed. Makes 4 servings.

STRAWBERRY PIE

Few shoppers can resist buying at least a few baskets of plump, red strawberries when they're in season. Here's a sumptuous way to celebrate this lovely fruit, perhaps as the sweet finale to a summer barbecue.

- 3 **baskets strawberries**
- 1 **cup sugar**
- 3 **tablespoons cornstarch**
- 1 **tablespoon butter or margarine, cut into pieces**
- 9-**inch baked pastry shell, 1½ inches deep, in a glass, ceramic, or plastic dish**
  Whipped cream (optional)

Wash and hull berries; cut enough berries in half to make 4 cups total. Set remaining whole berries aside.

In a 2-quart batter bowl or casserole, stir together the 4 cups cut strawberries, sugar, cornstarch, and butter. Cover with wax paper. Microwave on **HIGH (100%)** for 6 to 7 minutes (stirring every 3 minutes) or until mixture boils and thickens.

Pour into baked pastry shell; let cool completely. Top with whole strawberries and refrig-

erate. Before serving, top with whipped cream, if desired. Makes 6 servings.

SUGARLESS APPLE PIE

If you prefer to serve your family naturally sweetened desserts, try this apple pie that uses the fruity sugar of apple juice rather than refined sugar. Embellish the servings, if you wish, with whipped cream, ice cream, or Cheddar cheese.

- 1 **can (12 oz.) frozen apple juice concentrate, thawed**
- 3 **tablespoons cornstarch**
- ¼ **teaspoon salt**
- 1 **teaspoon ground cinnamon**
- ½ **teaspoon ground nutmeg**
- 5 **or 6 large Golden Delicious apples, peeled, cored, and sliced ¼ inch thick (6 cups)**
- 2 **tablespoons firm butter or margarine**
- 9-**inch baked pastry shell, 1½ inches deep, in glass, ceramic, or plastic dish**
  Whipped cream, ice cream, or Cheddar cheese slices (optional)

In a 2-quart batter bowl or casserole, stir together apple juice, cornstarch, salt, cinnamon, and nutmeg; blend well, then stir in apples. Cut butter into small pieces and dot over apples. Cover with wax paper. Microwave on **HIGH (100%)** for 8 minutes, stirring after 4 minutes. Uncover and microwave on **HIGH (100%)** for 8 more minutes, stirring after 4 minutes. Apple slices should be fork-tender. Let cool, uncovered, for 20 to 30 minutes before spooning into baked pastry shell.

Refrigerate before serving. Serve with whipped cream, ice cream, or slices of Cheddar cheese, if desired. Makes 6 to 8 servings.

SPICY PUMPKIN PIE

(Pictured on opposite page)

Don't think pumpkin pie is only holiday fare — with canned pumpkin readily available, you can make this creamy, deliciously spicy pie the year around.

- 3 **eggs**
- ⅓ **cup *each* granulated sugar and firmly packed brown sugar**
- ½ **teaspoon salt**
- 1½ **teaspoons ground cinnamon**
- 1 **teaspoon ground ginger**
- ½ **teaspoon ground cloves**
- 2 **cans (5⅓ oz. each) evaporated milk**
- 1 **can (16 oz.) pumpkin**
- 10-**inch baked pastry shell, 1½ inches deep, in glass, ceramic, or plastic dish**

In a 2-quart glass measure or bowl, beat eggs lightly. Add granulated sugar, brown sugar, salt, cinnamon, ginger, cloves, and evaporated milk; beat until well blended. Beat in pumpkin until mixture is smooth and thoroughly mixed.

Microwave, uncovered, on **HIGH (100%)** for 6 to 7 minutes (stirring with a wire whip every 2 minutes) or until mixture thickens slightly. Pour into baked pastry shell.

Microwave, uncovered, on **MEDIUM (50%)** for 12 to 15 minutes, rotating plate ¼ turn every 5 minutes. Filling should jiggle slightly in center when plate is gently shaken. (Upon standing, center will set.)

Let stand, uncovered, for 1 hour; or cover loosely with plastic wrap and refrigerate. Makes 6 to 8 servings.

A harvest season favorite, Spicy Pumpkin Pie (recipe above) once took the harried holiday cook more than an hour to prepare. Now you can bake the crust conventionally while the custard is in the microwave; then assemble the pie and bake it to perfection in under 15 minutes.

CREAM CHEESE PIE

For an easy dessert that will draw rave reviews, try this simple but super-tasting cheesecake.

For best results, chill for at least four hours before serving. And since this pie has an egg-based filling, it should always be refrigerated.

> 6 **tablespoons butter or margarine**
> 1½ **cups graham cracker crumbs (about 18 crackers)**
> 4 **small packages (3 oz. *each*) cream cheese, softened**
> ⅔ **cup sugar**
> ½ **pint (1 cup) sour cream**
> 2 **teaspoons vanilla**
> 2 **eggs**

Place butter in a 9-inch pie plate. Microwave, uncovered, on **HIGH (100%)** for 1 minute or until butter melts. Add cracker crumbs and stir to coat. Press mixture evenly over bottom and side of plate. Microwave, uncovered, on **HIGH (100%)** for 1 minute; set aside.

In a 2-quart glass measure or bowl, beat cream cheese and sugar until well blended. Beat in sour cream, vanilla, and eggs; blend well. Cover with wax paper. Microwave on **MEDIUM (50%)** for 7 minutes, beating with a wire whip every 2 minutes or until thickened. Pour hot egg mixture *gently* into prepared crust (otherwise, crust will crack).

Microwave, uncovered on **MEDIUM (50%)** for 3 to 6 minutes, rotating plate ¼ turn every 2 minutes. Filling should jiggle slightly in center when plate is gently shaken. (Upon standing, center will set.) Let stand for 20 minutes, then cover loosely with wax paper and refrigerate for at least 4 hours or overnight. Cut into small wedges to serve. Refrigerate any remaining pieces. Makes 10 to 12 servings.

CHEESECAKE TARTS

(Pictured on page 79)

These rich and creamy individual cheesecakes, made in advance and chilled, can rescue you from last-minute dessert worries. Brighten each tart with a generous spoonful of cherry pie filling just before serving.

> 3 **tablespoons butter or margarine**
> ½ **cup graham cracker crumbs**
> 1½ **teaspoons sugar**
> 1 **large package (8 oz.) cream cheese, softened**
> ¼ **cup sugar**
> 1 **egg**
> 1 **teaspoon vanilla**
> **Canned cherry pie filling**

Place butter in a 10-ounce custard cup. Microwave, uncovered, on **HIGH (100%)** for 1 minute. Blend in cracker crumbs and the 1½ teaspoons sugar.

Line six 6-ounce custard cups with paper baking cups; spoon crumb mixture equally into cups. With a spoon, press mixture firmly over bottom and slightly up sides of cups. Arrange cups in a circle on a large flat plate.

In a small bowl, beat cream cheese and the ¼ cup sugar until smooth. Beat in egg and vanilla, blending well. Spoon mixture equally into crumb-lined cups.

Microwave, uncovered, on **HIGH (100%)** for 2½ to 3½ minutes, rotating each cup ½ turn after 1½ minutes. Tarts should

look slightly dry on top. Let stand for 10 minutes on plate, then remove cups from plate and refrigerate for 1 hour. Remove tarts from cups (peel off paper liners, if desired) and serve; or cover and refrigerate. Just before serving, spoon cherry pie filling over each cheesecake. Makes 6 servings.

SWEDISH FRUIT SOUP

From Sweden, where hot and spicy fruit concoctions cheer away the winter chill, comes a most unusual dessert. Tangy with apples and cherries, as well as dried fruits, it's delicious hot or cold. Top each serving with a dollop of whipped cream, if you like.

> 6 **ounces pitted prunes**
> ½ **cup *each* golden seedless raisins and dried apricots**
> 2 **medium-size tart apples (peeled, if desired), cored and cut into ¼-inch slices**
> **3-inch cinnamon stick**
> 2 **cups water**
> ½ **cup sugar**
> 1 **can (1 lb.) pitted sweet cherries**
> 4 **teaspoons cornstarch**
> **Whipped cream (optional)**

In a 2-quart casserole, place prunes, raisins, apricots, apples, and cinnamon stick. Add water and sugar; stir to blend. Cover with a lid or plastic wrap. Microwave on **HIGH (100%)** for 12 to 15 minutes (stirring every 5 minutes) or until apples are fork-tender. Add cherries, reserving juice. Stir cornstarch into juice and blend well; then add to hot fruit mixture and stir gently.

Microwave, covered, on **HIGH (100%)** for 2 to 4 minutes (stirring after every minute) or until thickened. Fruits should retain their shapes. Makes 6 servings.

Serve hot. Or cool, cover, and refrigerate. Ladle into bowls and pass whipped cream at the table, if desired. Makes 5 or 6 1-cup servings.

APPLE CRISP

Spicy and delicious, this time-honored favorite is almost as American as apple pie. And with a microwave oven, it's also as easy. Crown servings with a dollop of whipped cream, a scoop of ice cream, or a slice of cheese, if you wish.

For a pleasing variation, use pears instead of apples.

- ¾ cup *each* all-purpose flour and firmly packed brown sugar
- ½ cup old-fashioned rolled oats
- 1½ teaspoons ground cinnamon
- ½ teaspoon ground nutmeg
- 6 tablespoons firm butter or margarine
- 6 cups (5 to 6 large) cored, peeled, and thinly sliced tart apples or firm ripe pears
- 1 tablespoon lemon juice
  Whipped cream, ice cream, or Cheddar cheese slices (optional)

In a small bowl, stir together flour, sugar, oats, cinnamon, and nutmeg. Cut butter into small pieces and, with a pastry blender or two forks, cut into flour mixture until crumbly; set aside.

In a 2-quart casserole, toss together apples and lemon juice. Sprinkle flour mixture over apples. Microwave, uncovered, on **HIGH (100%)** for 11 to 13 minutes (rotating dish ¼ turn after 5 minutes) or until apples are fork-tender. Let stand, uncovered, for 5 minutes before serving.

Serve warm. Or cool and refrigerate; bring to room temperature before serving. Top with whipped cream, ice cream, or cheese slices, if desired. Makes 5 or 6 servings.

CHERRIES JUBILEE

For sheer elegance with very little fuss, let cherries jubilee bring a candlelight dinner to a delicious conclusion.

- 1 bag (16 oz.) frozen unsweetened pitted dark sweet cherries, thawed
- 1 tablespoon cornstarch
- ⅓ cup currant jelly
- 2 tablespoons sugar
- ¼ cup kirsch (cherry brandy)
  About 1½ pints vanilla ice cream

Drain juice from cherries into a 1½ to 2-quart serving dish. Add cornstarch and stir until smooth. Stir in jelly and sugar; blend well. Microwave, uncovered, on **HIGH (100%)** for 2 to 3 minutes (stirring after 1½ minutes) or until sauce is thickened and clear. Stir in cherries and any additional juice. Cover with wax paper. Microwave on **HIGH (100%)** for 2 to 3 minutes (stirring every minute) or until heated through.

Place kirsch in a glass measure. Microwave, uncovered, on **HIGH (100%)** for 30 seconds. Pour over cherries and ignite (*not* beneath an exhaust fan or flammable items); then continuously spoon flaming sauce over cherries until flame dies. Spoon cherries and sauce over scoops of ice cream. Makes about 6 servings.

FLAMING BANANAS GUADALAJARA

A perfect accompaniment for this dessert would be a small mariachi band serenading you and your guests as you present this flaming treat.

- 3 tablespoons butter or margarine
- 3 tablespoons firmly packed brown sugar
  Dash of ground nutmeg
- ¼ teaspoon ground cinnamon
- 4 firm ripe bananas
- 2 tablespoons *each* rum and coffee-flavored liqueur
  About 1½ pints vanilla or coffee ice cream

Place butter in a shallow 1½ to 2-quart serving dish. Microwave, uncovered, on **HIGH (100%)** for 1 minute. Stir in sugar, nutmeg, and cinnamon. Microwave, uncovered, on **HIGH (100%)** for 1 to 2 minutes or until sugar dissolves. Peel bananas and cut into ½-inch-thick slices. Add to butter mixture and toss gently to coat. Cover with wax paper. Microwave on **HIGH (100%)** for 2 minutes or until bananas soften slightly.

In a glass measure, combine rum and coffee-flavored liqueur. Microwave, uncovered, on **HIGH (100%)** for 30 seconds. Pour over bananas and ignite (*not* beneath an exhaust fan or flammable items); then continuously spoon flaming sauce over bananas until flame dies. Spoon bananas and sauce over scoops of ice cream. Makes about 6 servings.

Sauces – Savory or Sweet

In cooking, the difference between the humdrum and the memorable can often be the crowning touch of a simple sauce. Whether it's a savory sauce for broccoli or meat loaf, or a sweet one for cake or ice cream, the right sauce can transform ordinary, familiar flavors into an extraordinary gourmet experience.

In this chapter you'll find saucy elegance ranging from the classics to the brand new. Making all of them is as effortless and instantaneous as you expect from a microwave. And best of all, the microwave eliminates the problems of sticking and scorching sometimes encountered in conventional cooking.

TIPS & TECHNIQUES

○ **Sauce utensils.** We like using a 4-cup glass measure for our sauces — its handle makes it easy to remove from the microwave for stirring, and its shape allows for even heating all around.

You'll want to have a wire whip on hand as you prepare sauce. Use it to blend the ingredients smoothly and to stir during the cooking process — stirring distributes the heat evenly and prevents lumps from forming.

○ **Thickening with cornstarch or flour.** Sauces thickened with cornstarch or flour must reach the boiling point to eliminate the raw taste of the starch. We use the same method for making a white sauce as you would conventionally — the fat is melted, the starch stirred in to make a roux, then both are heated until bubbly (the recipe for White Sauce is on page 91).

When liquid is added to the roux and the sauce begins to boil, you'll need to stir it with a wire whip every minute to keep the sauce smooth.

When you're adding cornstarch to fruit (as in the recipe for Raspberry or Strawberry Sauce on page 93) or stirring milk into a roux, look through the bottom of the glass measure to be sure all the cornstarch has been stirred into the liquid.

o **Thickening with egg yolk.** Sauces thickened with egg yolks, such as our Soft Custard Sauce on page 92, need constant attention and stirring to prevent the outside surfaces from curdling and overcooking. *Do not boil* sauces thickened with egg yolks or they will curdle.

o **Storing and reheating sauces.** For the ultimate in convenience, store all our sauces in glass jars and refrigerate. When you're ready to reheat and serve, simply remove the metal lid and put the jar in the microwave, or spoon the amount needed into a glass dish. Cover the container with wax paper to assure even distribution of heat during the reheating.

For all except egg-based sauces, microwave on **HIGH (100%)** for 1 minute per cup of sauce or until the sauce is heated through. Stir the sauce with a wire whip.

Egg-based sauces should be reheated on **MEDIUM (50%)** for 2 minutes (stirring after 1 minute, then at 30-second intervals) or until the sauce is heated through.

FLUFFY HORSERADISH SAUCE

(Pictured on page 23)

To embellish roast beef, pork, ham, or smoked tongue, offer a bowl of this cool, tangy sauce and let your guests help themselves. Or serve it as a spread for a do-it-yourself sandwich buffet.

2 egg yolks
2 tablespoons *each* white wine vinegar and prepared horseradish
1 tablespoon *each* sugar, Dijon mustard, and water
½ teaspoon salt
½ cup whipping cream

In a 2-cup glass measure, beat egg yolks lightly with a wire whip. Add vinegar, horseradish, sugar, mustard, water, and salt. Beat until well blended.

Microwave, uncovered, on **HIGH (100%)** for 2 minutes, beating with a wire whip after 1 minute. Cover and refrigerate.

Whip cream until soft, moist, peaks form. Beat cool horseradish mixture until smooth; fold into cream. Cover and refrigerate for up to 4 days. Serve cold. Makes about 1½ cups.

WHITE SAUCE

You'll appreciate the versatility of this basic white sauce — we offer four delightful variations, all of which take only minutes to prepare in the microwave. The roux is cooked on high until bubbly before the milk is added, resulting in a smooth and creamy sauce.

2 tablespoons butter or margarine
2 tablespoons all-purpose flour
½ teaspoon salt
1 cup milk

Place butter in a 4-cup glass measure. Microwave, uncovered, on **HIGH (100%)** for 1 minute. Stir in flour and salt to make a roux. Microwave, uncovered, on **HIGH (100%)** for 30 seconds or until bubbly. Gradually stir in milk; blend well. Microwave, uncovered, on **HIGH (100%)** for 3 to 3½ minutes (stirring every minute) or until sauce is bubbly and thickened. Makes about 1 cup.

Cheese sauce. Prepare White Sauce. Add ¾ cup shredded **Cheddar cheese** to hot sauce and stir until sauce is thickened and cheese is melted. Makes 1¼ cups.

Curry sauce. Prepare White Sauce, adding 1½ teaspoons **curry powder** and ⅛ teaspoon **ground ginger** with flour. Makes about 1 cup.

Dill sauce. Prepare White Sauce. Stir 2 teaspoons **dill weed,** 1 teaspoon chopped **parsley,** and ½ teaspoon **lemon juice** into hot sauce. Makes about 1 cup.

Green onion sauce. Prepare White Sauce, adding 1 teaspoon **dry mustard** and 3 tablespoons thinly sliced **green onions** (including tops) with flour. Makes about 1¼ cups.

TANGY BARBECUE SAUCE

For rich color and flavor, brush this sauce generously over chicken, turkey, roasts, spareribs, frankfurters, or hamburgers.

¾ cup tomato-based chili sauce
3 tablespoons water
2 tablespoons *each* cider vinegar and firmly packed brown sugar
2 teaspoons instant minced onion
1 teaspoon *each* prepared mustard and Worcestershire
½ teaspoon prepared horseradish

In a 2-cup glass measure, stir together chili sauce, water, vinegar, sugar, onion, mustard, Worcestershire, and horseradish.

Microwave, uncovered, on **HIGH (100%)** for 2 to 3 minutes (stirring every minute) or until bubbly.

Brush over meat or poultry the last third of the cooking time. Makes about 1¼ cups.

TOMATO SAUCE

Here's a fresh-looking and fresh-tasting sauce that's perfect over noodles, vermicelli, or ricotta-filled pasta. Shredded carrot sweetens the sauce and adds bright color.

- 1 small onion, finely chopped
- 1 stalk celery, finely chopped
- 1 medium-size carrot, shredded
- 1 clove garlic, minced or pressed
- 4 tablespoons olive oil or salad oil (or 2 tablespoons of *each*)
- 1 can (about 1 lb.) whole peeled tomatoes
- 1 tablespoon chopped fresh basil leaves or 1 teaspoon dry basil
- ¼ teaspoon white pepper
  Salt

In a 1-quart casserole, place onion, celery, carrot, and garlic. Stir in oil. Cover with wax paper. Microwave on **HIGH (100%)** for 4 minutes. Add tomatoes (break up with a spoon) and their liquid. Stir in basil and pepper. Microwave, uncovered, on **HIGH (100%)** for 9 to 12 minutes (stirring every 3 minutes) or until sauce has thickened and most of the juices have evaporated.

Remove about ¾ cup of the sauce and purée in a food processor or blender; return purée to sauce. Season to taste with salt. Reheat on **HIGH (100%)** for 2 minutes (stirring after 1 minute), if desired. Makes about 2 cups.

FRESH MUSHROOM SAUCE

This richly flavored mushroom sauce turns ground meat patties or poached fish fillets into company fare. It's equally good over freshly cooked vegetables or leftover meat loaf, roast beef, or turkey slices.

- 2 tablespoons butter or margarine
- ¼ pound mushrooms, sliced
- ¼ cup finely chopped onion
- 2 tablespoons all-purpose flour
- 1 chicken bouillon cube dissolved in ¾ cup hot water
- 1 tablespoon dry sherry
  White pepper and ground nutmeg

Place butter in a 1-quart casserole. Microwave, uncovered, on **HIGH (100%)** for 30 seconds or until melted. Stir in mushrooms and onion. Microwave, covered with wax paper, on **HIGH (100%)** for 3 minutes, stirring after 2 minutes. Stir in flour and microwave, uncovered, on **HIGH (100%)** for 30 seconds.

Gradually stir bouillon into mushroom mixture. Microwave, uncovered, on **HIGH (100%)** for 3½ to 4 minutes (stirring every minute) or until sauce boils and thickens. Stir in sherry and sprinkle with pepper and nutmeg to taste. Let stand, covered with wax paper, for 3 minutes to blend flavors. Makes 1¼ cups.

SOFT CUSTARD SAUCE

Spoon this mellow chilled sauce over slices of fresh fruit or chunks of pound cake.

- 3 tablespoons sugar
- 1 teaspoon cornstarch
  Dash of salt
- ¾ cup milk
- 3 egg yolks
- 1 teaspoon vanilla

In a 4-cup glass measure, stir together sugar, cornstarch, and salt. Gradually stir in milk. Microwave, uncovered, on **HIGH (100%)** for 2½ minutes or until mixture is slightly thickened. Do *not* boil.

In a small bowl, beat egg yolks until blended. Beating constantly, gradually add ¼ cup of the milk mixture to egg yolks, then return egg yolk mixture to hot milk mixture. Microwave, uncovered, on **MEDIUM (50%)** for 1 to 1½ minutes (stirring every 30 seconds) or until mixture coats back of a metal spoon. Stir in vanilla. Cool, cover, and refrigerate for at least 6 hours or overnight. Makes about 1 cup.

MARSHMALLOW MINT SAUCE

What's more refreshing than a hint of mint? You'll love this airy, light sauce over chocolate or rocky road ice cream.

- ¼ cup water
- ½ cup sugar
- ½ cup miniature marshmallows, or large marshmallows cut into quarters
- 1 egg white
- ⅛ teaspoon peppermint extract
  Green food coloring (optional)

In a 4-cup glass measure, stir together water and sugar. Microwave, uncovered, on **HIGH (100%)** for 1½ minutes or until boiling. Stir until sugar is completely dissolved.

Microwave, uncovered, on **HIGH (100%)** for about 2½ minutes (mixture should boil rapidly for at least 2 minutes) or until mixture forms a thin syrup. Add marshmallows and stir until melted; set aside to cool.

Beat egg white until stiff, moist peaks form. Beating constantly, gradually add cooled marshmallow mixture. Blend in peppermint. Stir in 1 or 2 drops of food coloring, if desired, to tint sauce pale green. Cover and refrigerate for up to a week. Stir well before serving. (Mixture will separate upon standing for a day or so — simply stir well before serving to regain creamy consistency.) Makes about 1½ cups.

ALMOND BUTTERSCOTCH SAUCE

An established favorite over vanilla ice cream, this rich sauce is just as delicious drizzled over warm apple turnovers or chilled baked custard.

- 1½ cups firmly packed brown sugar
- ½ cup whipping cream
- 3 tablespoons firm butter or margarine, cut into pieces
  Dash of salt
- ½ cup roasted slivered almonds (page 15)
- ½ teaspoon vanilla

In a 4-cup glass measure, stir together sugar, cream, butter, and salt. Microwave, uncovered, on **HIGH (100%)** for 2½ to 3 minutes (stirring every minute) or until mixture boils. Stir in almonds and vanilla. Let stand, covered with wax paper, for 10 to 15 minutes to thicken. Serve warm or at room temperature. Makes about 1⅔ cups.

CRANBERRY WALNUT SAUCE

Wonderfully spicy, this fruit and nut-laden sauce makes a distinguished accompaniment to turkey and chicken. Or try it for dessert, spooned over scoops of vanilla ice cream.

- 1 can (1 lb.) whole berry cranberry sauce
- ⅓ cup *each* sugar and water
- 1 cup golden raisins
- ½ teaspoon *each* ground cinnamon and grated lemon peel
- 2 tablespoons lemon juice
- ¼ teaspoon ground cloves
- ⅓ cup coarsely chopped walnuts

In a 4-cup glass measure, stir together cranberry sauce, sugar, water, raisins, cinnamon, lemon peel, lemon juice, and cloves. Microwave, uncovered, on **HIGH (100%)** for 6 minutes (stirring after 3 minutes) or until bubbly. Cool, cover, and refrigerate for up to 2 weeks.

Just before serving, stir in nuts. Makes 3 cups.

CHOCOLATE FUDGE SAUCE

Chocoholics in your family will want to try all three variations of this basic hot fudge. Served warm over ice cream, the flavor combinations are almost endless.

- 4 ounces semisweet chocolate
  About ½ cup evaporated milk
- 3 tablespoons sugar
  Dash of salt
- 1 teaspoon vanilla

Place chocolate in a 4-cup glass measure. Microwave, uncovered, on **HIGH (100%)** for 2 minutes or until melted. Stir well, then gradually stir in ½ cup of the milk, sugar, and salt. Microwave, covered with wax paper, on **HIGH (100%)** for 2 minutes (stirring every minute) or until bubbly and thickened. Stir in vanilla.

For thinner sauce, stir in 1 to 3 more tablespoons milk, 1 tablespoon at a time, until sauce reaches desired consistency. Serve warm. Makes about 1 cup.

Chocolate rum sauce. Prepare Chocolate Fudge Sauce, omitting vanilla. Stir in 1½ to 2 teaspoons **rum extract.** Makes about 1 cup.

Chocolate orange sauce. Prepare Chocolate Fudge Sauce, omitting vanilla. Stir in 1½ to 2 teaspoons **orange extract** and ½ teaspoon grated **orange peel.** Makes about 1 cup.

Chocolate peanut butter sauce. Prepare Chocolate Fudge Sauce, stirring ¼ cup **chunk-style peanut butter** into melted chocolate before adding remaining ingredients. Makes about 1¼ cups.

RASPBERRY OR STRAWBERRY SAUCE

Whatever your preference, you can whip up either raspberry or strawberry sauce in minutes using frozen presweetened berries. Both sauces thicken after they're refrigerated and are best served cold. They're delectable toppings for such treats as pancakes, French toast, sponge cake, and ice cream, just to name a few.

- 1 package (about 10 oz.) frozen presweetened raspberries or strawberries
- 1 tablespoon light corn syrup
- 2 teaspoons cornstarch

If berries are in a cardboard container with metal ends, remove one end from package and place container upright on a paper towel on floor of microwave. (If packed in plastic pouch, place it on a paper-lined plate.) Microwave, uncovered, on **HIGH (100%)** for 2 minutes or until almost thawed.

Empty berries into a 2-cup glass measure; break up chunks with a spoon. Stir in corn syrup and cornstarch; blend well. Microwave, uncovered, on **HIGH (100%)** for 3 to 5 minutes (stirring every 2 minutes) or until mixture begins to boil. Cool, cover, and refrigerate. Sauce thickens on cooling. Makes 1 cup.

INDEX

Acorn squash with fruit, 59
Almond butterscotch sauce, 93
Almond fudge torte, 78
Almonds & pine nuts, 15
Almond toffee, 84
Aluminum foil, 7, 72
Appetizers, 12–19
Apple, cinnamon baked, 44
Apple crisp, 89
Apple jam, 77
Apple pie, sugarless, 86
Applesauce chocolate cake, 80
Apricot & pineapple jam, 77
Apricot jam, 77
Apricots, with game hens, 38
Arrangement of food, 8
Artichoke nibbles, 13
Artichokes, steamed, 49
Asparagus, steamed, 49–50
Asparagus au gratin, 54
Asparagus vinaigrette, 19
Au gratin, asparagus, 54
Au gratin potato ramekins, 56
Avocado beef patties, 28

Baby bottle, heating, 11
Baby food, heating, 11
Bacon, 21, 22
Baked apple, cinnamon, 44
Baked beans supreme, 54
Baked custard, individual, 83
Baked eggs in hash, 65
Baked potato entrées, 57
Bananas Guadalajara, flaming, 89
Barbecue sauce, tangy, 91
Bars, dried fruit & nut, 81
Bars, nutty chocolate chip, 83
Basic puffy omelet, 65
Bean & beef enchiladas, 29
Bean dip, Mexican, 14
Beans, baked supreme, 54
Beans, green or wax, steamed, 50
Beans Mexican, chili, 45
Bean sprouts, steamed, 50
Bean soup, sweet & sour, 60
Beef
    avocado beef patties, 28
    baked eggs in hash, 65
    cheeseburger in a bun, 45
    glazed meat loaf, 27
    ground beef patties, 22
    hot dogs in buns, 44
    Italian meatballs, 27
    liver olé, 30
    one rib for two, 28
    patties, 22
    roast, 22
    super nachos dinner, 27
    sweetbreads in cream, 29
    sweet & sour franks, 16
    teriyaki meatballs, 17
    See also Beef recipes listed below
Beef & bean enchiladas, 29
Beef burgundy, 28
Beets, Harvard, 54
Beets, steamed, 50
Benedict, eggs, 67
Berry jam, 77
Beverages
    brandied mocha, 19
    café au lait, 19
    cider, heating, 11
    cocoa, heating instant, 10
    coffee, heating, 11
    cranberry glogg, 19
    tea, heating, 11
    tips & techniques, 13

Blueberry coffee cake, 78
Blueberry jam, 77
Blueberry-orange muffins, 73
Boiling water, 11
Bok choy (see Swiss chard), 53
Bouillon, hot, 13
Brandied mocha, 19
Brandy cream, sweetbreads in, 29
Bran muffins, ready-bake, 75
Breads, 73
Brittle, peanut, 84
Broccoli, steamed, 50
Brownies, chocolate, 81
Browning meat & poultry, 21
Brown sugar, softening hardened, 10
Brussels sprouts, steamed, 50
Bubbly cheese & crackers, 44
Bun, cheeseburger in a, 45
Buns, hot dogs in, 44
Burgundy, beef, 28
Butter, cashew, with turkey, 38
Butter, garlic, 53
Butter, spiced, 53
Butter or margarine, melting, 10
Butter or margarine, softening, 10
Butterscotch almond sauce, 93

Cabbage, creamy, 55
Cabbage, steamed, 50
Cabbage, sweet & sour red, 55
Café au lait, 19
Cake
    blueberry coffee, 78
    carrot, 80
    chocolate applesauce, 80
    sour cream coffee, 75
Canapés, 12
Candied walnuts, 85
Candies, 84–85
Carrot cake, 80
Carrots, orange-glazed, 54
Carrots, steamed, 50
Carrot-topped poached fish, 43
Cashew butter, with turkey, 38
Casserole
    chili relleno, 68
    dilled tuna, 46
    Mexican zucchini, 59
    reheating, 11
    turkey-tortilla, 41
Cauliflower, steamed, 51
Cheddar sauce, scallops in, 41
Cheese, melting, 12, 65
Cheese, softening refrigerated, 12
Cheese, tips & techniques, 65
Cheese & chili enchiladas, 68
Cheese & crackers, bubbly, 44
Cheese & ham-stacked potatoes, 57
Cheese & macaroni, 70
Cheese & mushroom sandwiches, 33
Cheeseburger in a bun, 45
Cheesecake tarts, 88
Cheese fondue, chilies in, 16
Cheese sandwich, grilled, 33
Cheese sauce, 91
Cheese sauce, quick, 53
Cheese topping, for cheeseburger in a
    bun, 45
Cherries jubilee, 89
Cherry jam, 77
Chestnuts, 15
Chicken
    breast, 25
    broiler-fryer, 25
    cornflake-coated, 40
    Kauai, 36
    legs, 25
    onion & sage-coated, 40
    oven-fried, 40
    paprika-coated, 40
    Parmesan-coated, 40

Chicken (cont'd.)
    stuffing-coated, 40
    Swiss, 36
    See also Chicken recipes listed by title
    below
Chicken curry, 37
Chicken divan ramekins, 37
Chicken in tarragon cream, 36
Chicken liver bundles, 16
Chicken with plum sauce, 37
Chili & cheese enchiladas, 68
Chili beans Mexicana, 45
Chilies-in-cheese fondue, 16
Chili relleno casserole, 68
Chocolate, melting, 10
Chocolate applesauce cake, 80
Chocolate brownies, 81
Chocolate chip bars, nutty, 83
Chocolate fudge, quick, 85
Chocolate fudge sauce, 93
Chocolate orange sauce, 93
Chocolate peanut butter sauce, 93
Chocolate rum sauce, 93
Chocolate truffles, 85
Chowder, clam & corn, 60
Cider, heating, 11
Cinnamon baked apple, 44
Citrus fruit, reaming juice, 10
Clam & corn chowder, 60
Clams with garlic butter, 17
Cocoa, heating instant, 10
Coffee, heating, 11, 13
Coffee cake, blueberry, 78
Coffee cake, sour cream, 75
Containers, microwave-safe, 6–7
Corn, quick Mexican, 55
Corn & clam chowder, 60
Cornflake-coated chicken, 40
Corn on the cob, steamed, 51
Country-style ribs, simmered, 32
Country vegetable soup, French, 61
Covering food, 7
Crab dip, hot, 17
Crab in spicy tomato sauce, 43
Crackers & bubbly cheese, 44
Cranberry glogg, 19
Cranberry walnut sauce, 93
Cream, brandy, sweetbreads in, 29
Cream, tarragon, chicken in, 36
Cream, zabaglione, 83
Cream cheese, softening, 10
Cream cheese frosting, with
    carrot cake, 80
Cream cheese pie, 88
Creamy cabbage, 55
Creamy dilled fish steaks, 46
Creamy scrambled eggs, 68
Crêpes, warming, 10
Crisp, apple, 89
Croutons, making, 11
Crunchy toppers, with vegetables, 53
Curry, chicken, 37
Curry sauce, 91
Custard, individual baked, 83
Custard sauce, soft, 92

Defrosting a pound of fish, 21
Defrosting food, 8–9
Dessert
    almond fudge torte, 78
    apple crisp, 89
    carrot cake, 80
    cheesecake tarts, 88
    cherries jubilee, 89
    chocolate applesauce cake, 80
    chocolate brownies, 81
    cream cheese pie, 88
    dried fruit & nut bars, 81
    flaming bananas Guadalajara, 89
    individual baked custard, 83
    nutty chocolate chip bars, 83

Dessert (cont'd.)
 spicy pumpkin pie, 86
 spicy steamed pudding, 80
 strawberry pie, 86
 sugarless apple pie, 86
 Swedish fruit soup, 88
 zabaglione cream, 83
Dilled fish steaks, creamy, 46
Dilled tuna casserole, 46
Dill sauce, 91
Dip, hot crab, 17
Dip, Mexican bean, 14
Dish test for microwave-safe utensils, 6
Dressing up the bird, 40
Dress up your vegetables, 53
Dried fruit & nut bars, 81
Duckling, 25
Dumplings & pork chops, 35

Egg & ham scramble, 67
Eggs, 64–70
 baked in hash, 65
 creamy scrambled, 68
 fried, 69
 omelet, basic puffy, 65
 poached, 69
 scrambled, 69
 tips & techniques, 64–65
 See also Egg recipes listed by title
  below
Egg salad filling, 67
Eggs Benedict, 67
Enchiladas, beef & bean, 29
Enchiladas, chili & cheese, 68

Fig & orange jam, spiced, 77
Fillings, for basic puffy omelet, 65
Finger towels, heating, 11
Fish
 carrot-topped poached, 43
 clams in the shell, 24
 clams with garlic butter, 17
 cooking chart, 24
 crab in spicy tomato sauce, 43
 crab in the shell, 24
 creamy dilled steaks, 46
 dilled tuna casserole, 46
 hot crab dip, 17
 lobster tails, 24
 mussels in the shell, 24
 oysters, shucked, 24
 oysters in the shell, 24
 scallops, 24
 scallops in Cheddar sauce, 41
 scampi, 46
 shrimp, 24
 steaks or fillets, 24
 tips & techniques, 21
 trout, whole, 24
 See also Fish recipe listed by title below
Fish in vegetable sauce, 43
Flaming bananas Guadalajara, 89
Fluffy horseradish sauce, 91
Fluffy scrambled eggs, 69
Foil, aluminum, 7, 72
Fondue, chilies-in-cheese, 16
Fondue, Italian-style, 70
Franks, sweet & sour, 16
French country vegetable soup, 61
French onion soup, 61
Fresh fruit jams, 76
Fresh mushroom sauce, 92
Fried eggs, 69
Fruit, with acorn squash, 59
Fruit & nut bars, dried, 81
Fruit jams, fresh, 76
Fruit soup, Swedish, 88
Fudge, quick chocolate, 85
Fudge almond torte, 78
Fudge sauce, chocolate, 93

Game hens, Rock Cornish, 25
Game hens with apricots, 38
Garlic butter, 53
Garlic butter, with clams, 17
Glazed meat loaf, 27
Glogg, cranberry, 19
Green onion sauce, 91
Green peas, seasoned, 59
Greens (kale & mustard), steamed, 51
Grilled cheese sandwich, 33
Guadalajara, flaming bananas, 89

Ham, orange-glazed, 32
Ham & cheese-stacked potatoes, 57
Ham quiche, 70
Happy hour mushrooms, 13
Harvard beets, 54
Hash, baked eggs in, 65
Hearty hot sandwiches, 33
Herb-cheese butter, with vegetable
  platter, 62
Herbed lamb shanks, 35
Herbs, with mushrooms, 55
Hollandaise sauce, 67
Honey, uncrystallizing, 10
Hors d'oeuvres, 12–19
Horseradish sauce, fluffy, 91
Hot crab dip, 17
Hot dogs in buns, 44
Hot hearty sandwiches, 33
Hot oatmeal, quick, 44
Hot tots, zucchini, 14

Ice cream, softening, 10
Individual baked custard, 83
Italian meatballs, 27
Italian-style fondue, 70

Jam, microwave, 76
Jam, uncrystallizing, 10
Jams, fresh fruit, 76–77
Jubilee, cherries, 89

Kale, steamed, 51
Kauai chicken, 36
Kids' Korner, 44–45

Lamb, leg of, 22
Lamb, Persian with peaches, 35
Lamb shanks, herbed, 35
Leeks, steamed, 51
Lemon sauce, for spicy steamed
  pudding, 81
Liver bundles, chicken, 16
Liver olé, 30
Lobster tails, 24

Macaroni & cheese, 70
Marshmallow mint sauce, 92
Meat, 27–36
 cooking chart, 22
 tips & techniques, 20–21
Meatballs, Italian, 27
Meatballs, teriyaki, 17
Meat loaf, glazed, 27
Medley, Oriental, 62
Melting butter or margarine, 10
Melting cheese, 65
Melting chocolate, 10
Mexicana, chili beans, 45
Mexican bean dip, 14
Mexican corn, quick, 55
Mexican zucchini casserole, 59
Microwave egg basics, 69
Microwave jam, 76
Microwave ovens, introduction to, 4–9
 defrosting food, 8–9
 determining wattage, 6
 foods not to microwave, 9
 how ovens cook food, 4–5
 how ovens differ, 5
 microwave penetration, 5
 power designations, 6

Microwave ovens (cont'd.)
 reheating food, 9
 safety, 5
 special cooking techniques, 7–8
 special oven features, 6
 test for evenness of heating, 8
 utensils & materials, 6–7
 why cook with microwaves, 4
Mint marshmallow sauce, 92
Mocha, brandied, 19
Morsels, vegetable, 14
Muffins, blueberry-orange, 73
Muffins, ready-bake bran, 75
Mushroom & cheese sandwiches, 33
Mushrooms, happy hour, 13
Mushrooms, spinach-stuffed, 13
Mushrooms, steamed, 51
Mushroom sauce, fresh, 92
Mushrooms with herbs, 55
Mushroom velvet soup, 61
Mussels in the shells, 24
Mustard greens, steamed, 51
Mustard sauce, for chicken liver
  bundles, 16

Nachos dinner, super, 27
Napa cabbage, steamed, 50
Nectarine or peach jam, 77
Nibbles, artichoke, 13
Nut & dried fruit bars, 81
Nuts & seeds, roasted, 15
Nutty chocolate chip bars, 83
Nutty topping, for muffins, 75

Oatmeal, quick hot, 44
Olé liver, 30
Omelet, basic puffy, 65
One rib for two, 28
Onion & sage-coated chicken, 40
Onions, steamed, 51
Onion soup, French, 61
Orange & purple plum jam, 77
Orange & spiced fig jam, 77
Orange-blueberry muffins, 73
Orange-glazed carrots, 54
Orange-glazed ham, 32
Oriental medley, 62
Oven-fried chicken, 40
Oysters, 24

Paper products, 7, 72
Paprika-coated chicken, 40
Parmesan, tomatoes, 62
Parmesan-coated chicken, 40
Parsnips, steamed, 52
Patties, avocado beef, 28
Peach & plum jam, 77
Peaches, with Persian lamb, 35
Peach or nectarine jam, 77
Peanut brittle, 84
Peas, seasoned green, 59
Peas, steamed, 52
Pepper cups, rice-stuffed, 56
Pepperoni pizza rounds, 16
Persian lamb with peaches, 35
Pie
 cream cheese, 88
 spicy pumpkin, 86
 strawberry, 86
 sugarless apple, 86
Pineapple & apricot jam, 77
Pizza rounds, pepperoni, 16
Plastic wrap, 7
Pleated plastic wrap, 7
Plum & peach jam, 77
Plum jam, 77
Plum sauce, with chicken, 37
Plum sauce, with pork loin, 30
Poached eggs, 69
Poached fish, carrot-topped, 43
Pockets, sausage & sauerkraut, 33

Pork
  bacon, 22
  egg & ham scramble, 67
  eggs Benedict, 67
  ham quiche, 70
  orange-glazed ham, 32
  pepperoni pizza rounds, 16
  roast, 22
  sausage & sauerkraut pockets, 33
  simmered country-style ribs, 32
  spareribs, 22
  spicy sausage sauté, 32
  See also Pork recipes listed below
Pork chops & dumplings, 35
Pork loin with plum sauce, 30
Potato entrées, baked, 57
Potatoes, ham & cheese-stacked, 57
Potatoes, sloppy-Joe-topped, 57
Potatoes, steamed, 52
Potatoes, stuffed, 56
Potato ramekins, au gratin, 56
Poultry, 36–41
  cooking chart, 25
  tips & techniques, 21
Power designations, 6
Pudding, spicy steamed, 80
Puffy omelet, basic, 65
Pumpkin & winter squash seeds, 15
Pumpkin pie, spicy, 86
Purple plum & orange jam, 77

Quiche, ham, 70
Quick cheese sauce, 53
Quick chocolate fudge, 85
Quick hot oatmeal, 44
Quick Mexican corn, 55

Raspberry or strawberry sauce, 93
Ratatouille, 56
Ready-bake bran muffins, 75
Red cabbage, sweet & sour, 55
Reheating, 9
  bread products, 73
  canned foods, 9
  plate of room-temperature food, 11
  refrigerated leftovers, 11
  sauces, 91
Rib for two, one, 28
Ribs, simmered country-style, 32
Rice-stuffed pepper cups, 56
Roasted nuts & seeds, 15

Sage-coated & onion chicken, 40
Salad, egg filling, 67
Salted cashews, 15
Salted peanuts, 15
Salted walnuts, 15
Salting vegetables, 33
Sandwich, grilled cheese, 33
Sandwiches, mushroom & cheese, 33
Sauce
  almond butterscotch, 93
  chocolate fudge, 93
  cranberry walnut, 93
  curry, 91
  dill, 91
  fluffy horseradish, 91
  fresh mushroom, 92
  green onion, 91
  hollandaise, 67
  lemon, 81
  marshmallow mint, 92
  quick cheese, 53
  raspberry or strawberry, 93
  soft custard, 92
  sour cream, 53
  tangy barbecue, 91
  thickening with cornstarch or flour, 90
  thickening with egg yolks, 91
  tips & techniques, 90–91
  tomato, 92
  white, 91

Sauerkraut & sausage pockets, 33
Sausage & sauerkraut pockets, 33
Sausage sauté, spicy, 32
Scallops, 24
Scallops in Cheddar sauce, 41
Scampi, 46
Scrambled eggs, creamy, 68
Scrambled eggs, fluffy, 69
Seasoned green peas, 59
Seeds & nuts, roasted, 15
Shanks, herbed lamb, 35
Shielding with foil, 72
Shrimp, 24
Simmered country-style ribs, 32
Sloppy-Joe-topped potatoes, 57
S'mores, 45
Soft custard sauce, 92
Softening butter or margarine, 10
Softening cream cheese, 10
Softening hardened brown sugar, 10
Softening ice cream, 10
Softening refrigerated cheese, 12
Soup
  clam & corn chowder, 60
  French country vegetable, 61
  French onion, 61
  heating prepared, 11
  mushroom velvet, 61
  Swedish fruit, 88
  sweet & sour bean, 60
Sour cream coffee cake, 75
Sour cream sauce, 53
Spareribs, 22
Spiced butter, 53
Spiced fig & orange jam, 77
Spicy pumpkin pie, 86
Spicy sausage sauté, 32
Spicy steamed pudding, 80
Spicy tomato sauce, crab in, 43
Spinach, steamed, 52
Spinach-stuffed mushrooms, 13
Squash, acorn, with fruit, 59
Squash, steamed, 52
Squash, winter, 11, 52
Stale snacks, crisping, 12–13
Standing time, 8
Steamed pudding, spicy, 80
Stirring, rotating & rearranging, 8
Strawberry jam, 77
Strawberry or raspberry sauce, 93
Strawberry pie, 86
Stuffed potatoes, 56
Stuffing-coated chicken, 40
Sugarless apple pie, 86
Summer squash, steamed, 52
Sunflower seeds, 15
Super nachos dinner, 27
Swedish fruit soup, 88
Sweet & sour bean soup, 60
Sweet & sour franks, 16
Sweet & sour red cabbage, 55
Sweetbreads in brandy cream, 29
Sweet potatoes, steamed, 52

Sweets & breakfast treats, 72–89
  tips & techniques, 72–73
Swiss chard, steamed, 52
Swiss chicken, 36

Tangy barbecue sauce, 91
Tarragon cream, chicken in, 36
Tarts, cheesecake, 88
Tea, heating, 11, 13
Teriyaki, turkey legs, 41
Teriyaki meatballs, 17
Teriyaki sauce, with meatballs, 17
Tips & techniques
  eggs & cheese, 64–65
  hors d'oeuvres & beverages, 12–13
  meat, poultry & fish, 20–21
  miscellaneous, 10–11
  sauces—savory or sweet, 90–91
  sweets & breakfast treats, 72–73
  vegetables, 48–49
Toffee, almond, 84
Tomatoes Parmesan, 62
Tomato-herb sauce, for chili relleno
    casserole, 68
Tomato sauce, 92
Tomato sauce, spicy, crab in, 43
Torte, almond fudge, 78
Tortillas, warming, 10
Tortilla-turkey casserole, 41
Truffles, chocolate, 85
Tuna casserole, dilled, 46
Turkey
  breast half, 25
  drumsticks, 25
  testing internal temperature, 21
  whole, 25
  See also Turkey recipes listed below
Turkey legs teriyaki, 41
Turkey-tortilla casserole, 41
Turkey with cashew butter, 38
Turnips, steamed, 52

Uncrystallizing honey or jam, 10
Utensils, microwave-safe, 7

Veal roast, 22
Vegetable morsels, 14
Vegetable platter with herb-cheese
    butter, 62
Vegetables, 48–62
  cooking chart, 49–52
  tips & techniques, 48–49
Vegetable sauce, fish in, 43
Vegetable soup, French country, 61
Velvet mushroom soup, 61
Vinaigrette, asparagus, 19

Walnut cranberry sauce, 93
Walnuts, candied, 85
Wax-paper-lined dishes, 72
White sauce, 91

Zabaglione cream, 83
Zucchini casserole, Mexican, 59
Zucchini hot tots, 14

METRIC CONVERSION TABLE

To change	To	Multiply by
ounces (oz.)	grams (g)	28
pounds (lbs.)	kilograms (kg)	0.45
teaspoons	milliliters (ml)	5
tablespoons	milliliters (ml)	15
fluid ounces (fl. oz.)	milliliters (ml)	30
cups	liters (l)	0.24
pints (pt.)	liters (l)	0.47
quarts (qt.)	liters (l)	0.95
gallons (gal.)	liters (l)	3.8
Fahrenheit temperature (°F)	Celsius temperature (°C)	5/9 after subtracting 32